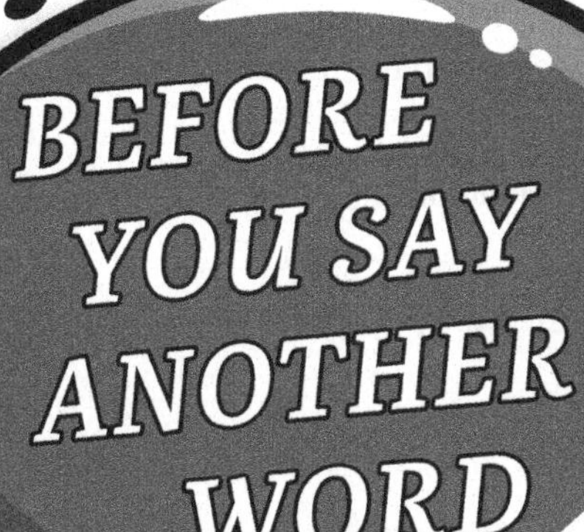

Thinking on Your Feet In Moments That Matter

DAVE MINIONIS, PhD

Before You Say Another Word: Thinking on Your Feet In Moments that Matter

Published by Humanetrics, LLC

Cover and Interior Design: GKS Creative

Editorial: Kim Bookless

Project Management: The Cadence Group

Paperback ISBN: 978-1-7358684-0-0

eISBN: 978-1-7358684-1-7

This book may be purchased for educational, business, or sales promotional use. For information, please email Dave@humanetricstraining.com or call 703-517-4121.

This book is dedicated to my father,
Roger V. Minionis. His natural ability to effortlessly think in the moment while maintaining confidence, poise, and likeability made him an inspirational teacher, a loving husband, an adored father and grandfather, and a role model to all his family, friends, and colleagues.

Contents

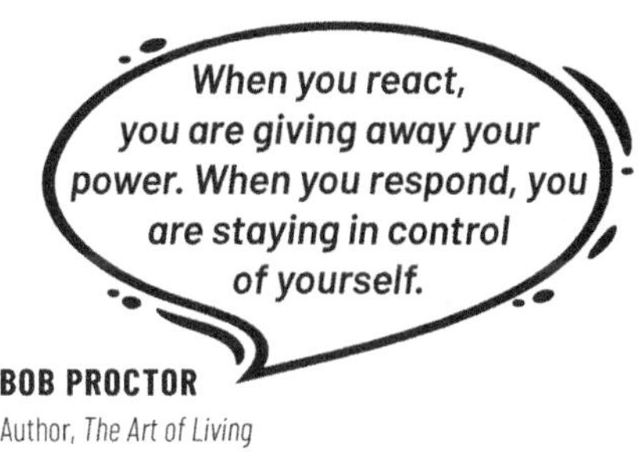

BOB PROCTOR
Author, *The Art of Living*

introduction

Before You Say Another Word

Thinking on Your Feet In Moments That Matter

IT'S AN UNSCRIPTED WORLD

A thinking-on-your-feet moment . . .

You're giving an update to community leaders on your response to an important and controversial issue. You have practiced, prepped several key stakeholders, and feel good about your opportunity to shine.

You begin your presentation and things seem to be moving along well when someone on the panel raises their hand and asks several argumentative questions: *"Why did it take so long to get this project started?" "Why are we constantly fixing broken systems?"*

YIKES!

Suddenly your moment is upended. Your heart starts pounding, your stomach churns, and your mind begins to race as you struggle to answer these "off the script" questions. How do you respond, maintain your credibility, and get back to the subject at hand?

What do I do?
What do I say?
How do I say it?
What if my mind goes blank?

This is a common occurrence we have all confronted, try to avoid, and usually dread. Whether you're put on the spot while attending a meeting, presenting a proposal, selling an idea, or answering a barrage of questions after a presentation, conveying your thoughts and being able to think on your feet in unexpected situations is a skill worth mastering. After all, wouldn't it be great to believe that you could deal with pretty much any situation thrown your way?

This is a real challenge for most people. Too often, they react off the cuff, preparing an answer before the questioner finishes their thought. That is, if they're not dumbstruck and silenced by the comment. So, how do you come across as understanding, articulate, persuasive, and credible?

Think what it would mean if you could master the skill of being cool on your feet, providing an organized and intelligent response that would instill confidence and trust with the people you encounter. Odds are good you'd have a renewed sense of self-confidence and conviction, no matter how aggressive your audience is in those unexpected moments.

There's no getting around it. We live in an unscripted world.

Even if you're someone who thrives on advance preparation, there will be plenty of times in your life when you won't have a well-thought-out preplanned answer or a standard response or pitch.

You can prepare for a whole range of questions, rehearse in front of the mirror, plan your facial expressions and precise wording until you deliver perfectly—for that job interview, important meeting, or career-advancing networking situation. But the minute there's another person involved, the script, wording, and facial expressions go out the window. How do you come across crisply and feel comfortable on the spot?

If you want to make an impression, you have to be able to cast yourself into the moment and think on your feet.

If you want to make an impression, you have to be able to cast yourself into the moment and think on your feet.

Some twenty or thirty years ago, most professional job ads required candidates to demonstrate "excellent verbal and written communication skills." They still do, but now employers are looking for more. Leaders are seeking team members who respond well under pressure, are organized in their thinking, and can communicate ideas in the moment. They know and can sense how sharp someone is by how thoughtfully and clearly they respond in a pressured setting. It's a real skill. Some people are naturals. If you're like me, it needs to be learned.

Most of the circumstances I discuss in this book apply both to public speaking and to those unanticipated and difficult one-on-one situations. At the same time, the principles discussed here also apply to informal relationships with family, friends, community groups, and all human interactions.

If you turn to the research, it shows that roughly 90 percent of all verbal communication in business is impromptu rather than formal, prepared presentations. The vast majority of the time, individuals will find themselves having to speak in unplanned situations, such as with the boss for a "quick update," a client calling unexpectedly to complain, the CEO wanting to discuss strategy, or your teenager deciding to sabotage your vacation plans. What's required is the ability to think fast and respond in the moment.

My Own Script Gone Awry

The first time I was sucker punched with words I didn't expect was at the age of twenty-four. It was a beautiful, sunny afternoon, six months into my first job as a recruiter for a large insurance company in New Jersey, I told my supervisor I was interested in growing my career and moving into a more leadership-focused position in the company. After all, I had worked very hard, spending long hours reviewing resumes and taking time to understand my clients' needs in order to fill their vacancies. There was nothing I wouldn't do for the company's success, and it showed in my positive, can-do attitude every single day.

When my boss called me into his office, I expected her to say, "We're thrilled you want to grow your career here. You've been such a valuable employee. Your clients love working with you and respect your opinion; the Human Resources team enjoys collaborating and brainstorming new ideas with you; and the staff appreciates the energy and humor you bring in to those long hours conducting campus interviews." I was ready to get my kudos and be welcomed into the next stage of my career.

But, shocking to me, my supervisor's reaction was exactly the opposite of my expectation. From behind her big desk, she said, "So what makes you think you have any of the skills, experience, or talent you need to be a leader here? You're not very organized and don't keep good notes. You're great at assessing people and promoting the company. However, you are more of an order taker than someone who thinks strategically."

Wow! My head exploded. To say I was shocked would be an understatement. Sucker punched! Big time. I could barely breathe, much less respond. I sat in stunned silence, and when I could finally compose myself and preserve some personal dignity, I got up and walked back to my desk, tail firmly placed between my legs.

My thinking on my feet moment passed. I sat and stewed, reliving every word and imagining every possible response I might have made. I felt powerless and defeated.

Fortunately, my racing mind found solace in a lecture my dad gave me thousands of times growing up. And until this moment, I didn't get it. But suddenly, it was like music to my ears. He said, "Always remember: Only you control your destiny. Never let anyone decide what your future will be. And the sooner you take control of your destiny, the sooner you will have the destiny you deserve."

I embraced those words and took control of my own personal destiny. Five months later, I was the top admissions officer for an independent IT training school in the Washington, DC, area.

A hard lesson was learned that day. I came to understand that every interaction is an opportunity to understand another perspective, learn something new, and respond in ways that allow me to take some control of the moment and move things in a direction I can control. Thinking on your feet is required in every situation. With your kids, your spouse, your boss, your colleagues. By learning to apply the key principles of thinking on your feet, you can develop a rich communication style that helps you build and maintain excellent relationships and move the world ever so slightly in your direction.

Lessons from Steve Jobs

Although my own thinking-on-your-feet story was a bust, Apple co-founder Steve Jobs repeatedly showed his mastery of being in the moment, thinking through a response, and projecting confidence and poise while interacting with some of the most demanding audiences on both good days and bad.

Here's a favorite. In 1997, Steve Jobs had just returned to Apple, the company he founded and was then asked to leave more than a decade earlier. Now back at the helm, he was answering questions at Apple's Worldwide Developers Conference when one audience member took this opportunity to publicly insult him. The result is one of the most quintessential thinking-on-your-feet interactions. And there's a lot we can learn from his template.

It begins: *"Mr. Jobs, you're a bright and influential man."*

"Here it comes," responds Jobs out loud, as both he and the audience get a little chuckle.

Then, the famous insult:

"It's sad and clear that on several counts you've discussed, you don't know what you're talking about. I would like, for example, for you to express in clear terms how, say, Java and any of its incarnations addresses the ideas embodied in OpenDoc. And when you're finished with that, perhaps you can tell us what you personally have been doing for the last seven years."

Ouch.

For most, a public thrashing like this might feel like a sucker punch—a punch so quick and hard that most any speaker would become flustered and knocked off balance. But, as it turned out, Jobs seemed to have been well schooled in the art of thinking on your feet.

He Pauses

The first thing Jobs does is probably the hardest.

He takes a pause, sits in silence . . . and continues to gather his thoughts.

In what seemed like an eternity (and in reality lasted about ten seconds, which is very much an eternity in front of thousands of followers), Jobs takes a sip of water and reflects on both the criticism and the question.

"You know," he begins his reply and buys some time. *"You can please some of the people some of the time, but . . ."*

Another pause, this time for about eight seconds.

These pauses are perhaps a subconscious way for him to gain the time he needed to compose himself and come back with a thoughtful and remarkable response.

He Agrees with His Accuser

"One of the hardest things when you're trying to effect change is that . . . people—like this gentleman—are right! . . . in some areas," explains Jobs.

It's always a good idea to start with a friendly response, even if you totally disagree with the other person's stance. In fact, research has shown that the best way to change a person's mind is not to attack their position but rather to find common ground.

> ***It's always a good idea to start with a friendly response. The best way to change a person's mind is not to attack their position but rather to find common ground.***

Jobs does this perfectly by acknowledging that this man is right . . . *"in some areas."*

He Answers the Question He Would Have Preferred

The question he got was about a specific programming language and his personal life. Instead of answering the technical question, he took it up a notch and responded to what could be considered the broader issue: *"Were mistakes made when we made those big technical changes in the company?"*

Jobs focuses on the big picture and outlines his role at Apple. From his perspective, it's not to know the ins and outs of every piece of software. Rather, it's to see the big picture, to reiterate the vision, and to keep everyone on course. He says:

"The hardest thing is: How does that fit into a cohesive larger vision that's going to allow you to sell eight billion dollars, ten billion dollars of product a year? And one of the things I've always found is that you've got to start with the customer experience and work backwards to the technology. You can't start with the technology and try to figure out where you're going to try to sell it."

This extremely compelling vision of working backwards from customer experience was a more innovative way of thinking at the time. And as history has proven, particularly at Apple, he was spot on.

He Shows Vulnerability, Admitting His Own Mistakes

In reference to working back to the customer, Jobs continues: *"And I've made this mistake probably more than anybody else in this room. And I've got the scar tissue to prove it. And I know that it's the case."*

Jobs not only explains his vision, he uses his own learnings to help establish his credibility, offering others the ability to benefit from his experience.

He Praises His Team

Jobs finishes strong in his response by pointing out there are people working long shifts, well past midnight, to crank out the application programs they think fit with their company's values, and that hard work is deserving of support and praise.

"There are a whole lot of people working super, super hard right now at Apple," Jobs exclaims. He names a few examples before going on to credit the whole team.

With these words, Jobs gets behind his team. He acknowledges them. He praises them.

He lets them know he's got their backs. And his genuine praise inspires the team (and others) to get behind him, too.

He Finishes Strong

Jobs's final words are motivating.

"Some mistakes will be made, by the way. And that's good. Because at least some decisions are being made along the way. And we'll find the mistakes, and we'll fix them," Jobs says to applause. *"And I think what we need to do is support that team going through this very important stage as they work their butts off . . ."*

He then comes full circle to the original questioner:

"Mistakes will be made . . . some people will not know what they're talking about, but I think it is so much better than where things were not very long ago.

"And I think we're going to get there."

The Takeaway

Whether it's a simple question, a conflicting comment, or an unexpected insult, how you handle yourself builds your credibility and develops trust. Take control of the moment and there is a greater chance you will move the conversation in your direction.

(Note: Many of these Steve Jobs lessons were highlighted in the "Business Insider" article by Justin Bariso of *Inc.* magazine and by Layla Tabatabaie in *FairyGodBoss* blog.)

HOW IT ALL BEGAN

I was involved with leadership development at a large healthcare insurance company when my co-faciliator and I were approached by management with a high-priority request. It seemed that when key managers were unexpectedly challenged in important meetings or conversations, they had difficulty responding well on the spot. The result was a loss of credibility and trust. Could we develop a program to help them gain credibility and clout when they're confronted? With that, we developed a *Thinking on Your Feet* workshop that is the inspiration for this book and the *Pause! Then Apply CPR* model revealed in Part 2.

GET READY TO BE READY

That's what this book is about. Being ready in the moment, when your credibility is challenged and when it matters most. If you read, reread, and apply the ideas and concepts in this book, when that moment comes, you will master the concepts by using the four learning strategies below:

Manage your anxiety and fear. No, your nervousness won't go away completely, but you will find ways to manage your anxiety and maximize it to help you handle the moment with poise and confidence.

Adapt to curveballs. It's going to happen: in a meeting, interview, casual interaction, surprise directive from your boss. Be ready to adapt and dazzle.

Develop your own thinking-on-your-feet framework to Pause! Then apply CPR (Clarify, Process, and Respond) so it becomes your natural inclination in spontaneous and tough situations.

Calmly respond, not react, when the moment is tense and the stakes are high. Respond with agility and flexibility, welcoming open discussion, building bridges, and forming relationships.

The book is divided into three parts:

Part 1: Take a Deep Breath

Let's take a look at the big picture of thinking on your feet. What does it actually look like? Now, just inhale, compose yourself, and plow forward.

Part 2: PAUSE! Then Apply CPR

At its core, thinking on your feet requires clarity, simplicity, and a crisp response. Discover the magic formula: Pause! Then apply CPR (Clarify, Process, and Respond).

Part 3: Now You're Killin' It!

The curveballs keep coming. Apply a new approach to impromptu situations, the insults, the negativity, and even the compliments that come your way. Put it all together for success in every situation.

Make It Real Worksheets

At the end of every chapter, you'll find a *Make It Real Worksheets* section that highlights some of the key points from the chapter and provides worksheets and exercises to help you apply the learning to your own situation and circumstances. Research shows that you are ten times more likely to remember something new if you take action immediately that reinforces the concept. Take it to heart. Before you go on to the next chapter, spend a few minutes on the exercises. Guaranteed, this step will help you learn, retain, and apply the principles with greater success.

Choose Your Own Adventure

Throughout the book, you will be presented with a variety of techniques and ideas. Some might even seem to contradict each other. That's because people have different styles and success factors.

Sometimes, the same things work differently for different people. Choose the techniques that work best for you. Focus on improving your own style, in your own way.

At the end of this book, on page 152, you'll find a form titled "Top 10 Things to Keep in Mind When Thinking on My Feet." Fill it in as you go along. When you find a concept or idea that speaks to you, add it to the list and include the page number so you can refer to it later. Make this your personal list for brilliantly thinking on your feet.

SUMMARY

Whether you're put on the spot while attending a meeting, presenting a proposal, selling an idea, or answering a barrage of questions after a presentation, being able to think on your feet in unexpected situations is a skill worth mastering.

Every interaction is an opportunity to understand another perspective and get closer to a better solution. Thinking on your feet with your kids, your spouse, your boss, or colleagues is the key to building and maintaining excellent relationships. Once achieved, you will have a renewed sense of self-confidence and the formula for interpersonal success.

MAKE IT REAL WORKSHEETS

Your Story. Your Motivation.

You're probably reading this book because at some time in the past, you've been caught unprepared in the moment. You've experienced conversations, meetings, presentations, or personal interactions where you were hit with a curveball, only to stammer and walk away frustrated, thinking of all the could haves, should haves and wish-I-hads . . .

The key moment for responding with thoughtful confidence, wisdom, and clarity had passed. An opportunity was missed. And you vowed to not let that happen again!

We can learn from our mistakes only if we face them, look them squarely in the eye, evaluate what happened, and recognize our flaws. As Dr. Phil loves to say, "You can't fix what you don't acknowledge."

So, get ready to face your story, one that possibly makes you cringe but will give you the motivation to acknowledge your imperfections and manage a few small tweaks that will make a great impact and change how you think on your feet forever.

Find Your Story

Think back. Describe a time when you were in a conversation, in a meeting, giving a presentation, or asked to jump in with your take on a situation, and instead of responding like the smart, experienced, knowledgeable, and confident person you are, you stammered, rambled, and fumbled your way through, feeling embarrassed and disappointed.

Describe the situation: the setting, people involved, topic/issue, comments, questions, requests made.

How did you respond? What did you say?

How did you say it? Describe your tone, body language, eye contact, etc.

What did you do well?

Lessons learned: In retrospect, what could you have changed to improve your reaction and response?

PART
1
Take a
Deep Breath

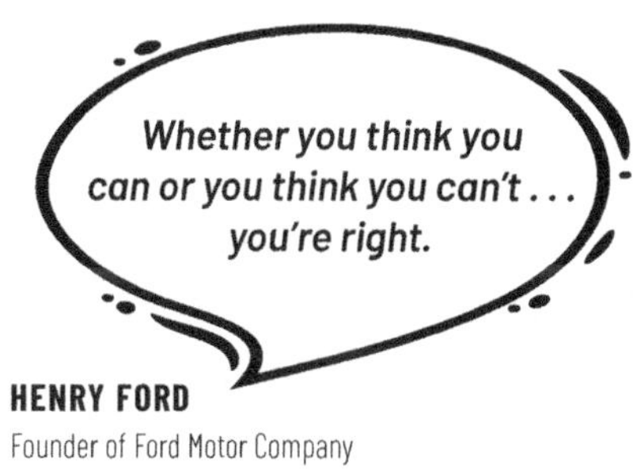

HENRY FORD
Founder of Ford Motor Company

Chapter 1

How the Masters Do It

What does excelling at thinking on your feet look like? Close your eyes and think about it. Picture someone you believe excels at thinking on their feet. Imagine them speaking, responding to questions, handling a difficult interaction. They are poised and articulate, engendering trust and confidence in the listener. They might be in front of a large audience, in a small meeting, or in a one-on-one conversation. Even when things are not going as expected, they handle the situation like a pro. Imagine their use of eye contact, their stance, body movement, voice, and facial expressions. What other successful behaviors and characteristics do they exhibit?

LEARN FROM THE BEST

Obviously, you and I know different people, so let's focus on some well-known names—people known for being good communicators and great at thinking on their feet (among their other skills and talents). I've come up with four: Stephen Colbert, host of *The Late Show With Stephen Colbert*; Sheryl Sandberg, activist and COO of Facebook; Robin Williams, actor and comedian extraordinaire;

and Melinda Gates, international philanthropist. You may come up with others, so feel free to add them to the list or replace any of these names with your own ideas and personal network. Now, look at the list below. Check off the characteristics those people successfully demonstrate when they are speaking, presenting, responding, negotiating, or engaged in a conversation:

- Articulation of ideas
- Authenticity
- Awareness
- Calmness
- Clarity of words
- Collaboration
- Confidence
- Empathy
- Enthusiasm
- Energy
- Good eye contact
- Good listening
- Humor
- Knowledge
- Open facial expression
- Passion
- Positive attitude
- Smart thinking
- Storytelling
- Thoughtfulness
- Voice modulation
- Warmth

It's likely that the people you chose to analyze, if they are truly great communicators, exhibit most if not all of the characteristics listed here. This tells us that successful communicators apply their own art to what research and science has taught us about human dynamics. It's no different than any personal interaction . . . only sometimes the stakes are higher.

In all instances, good communicators build connectivity. They show empathy, warmth, intelligence, and passion. But the biggest factors are confidence and likeability.

In all instances, good communicators build connectivity. They show empathy, warmth, intelligence, and passion.

Cool Confidence

Conveying confidence is important for many reasons but mostly because confidence is often equated with competence.

A confident speaker is passionate and warm, which fosters a connection with and respect from his or her audience. Ultimately, your confidence gives you credibility and garners support for your ideas and initiatives. A confident speaker who can carefully listen, articulate their ideas, and thoughtfully respond is seen as authentic, knowledgeable, and smart.

Confident passion comes from the energy and enthusiasm that a speaker exudes, as well as from the words they use. Passion must be real. Your energy and feelings must be authentic. Let the audience feel your positive energy when you look them in the eye. But be sure your emotions reflect your true feelings and are appropriate for the situation.

Let the audience feel your positive energy when you look them in the eye.

Researchers, such as popular TED presenter and Harvard Business

School professor Dr. Amy Cuddy, have shown that warmth is another key trait of confident, successful presenters. Warm behavior is a form of empathy. It is a combination of understanding your audience's needs and displaying that understanding through your actions.

By effectively conveying your passion, you demonstrate both your confidence and belief in yourself. You show your audience that you are authentic in your intent and committed to your message. And in return, you receive that same warmth back.

Arnold Schwazenegger Proves the Point

You must see it. You must believe it. And then you must never stop working to make it happen.

—Arnold Schwarzenegger

Arnold Schwarzenegger may not be the model of the spontaneous speaker, but he has natural abilities that have helped him be successful in spite of coming from a poor family in a small village in Austria and having little formal education.

With his goal set on using bodybuilding as his platform for immigrating to America, at age twenty Arnold became the youngest man to win the prestigious Mr. Universe competition.

As a result of his bodybuilding success, in 1977 Arnold was featured in a documentary called *Pumping Iron*. Surprising everyone at the end of the competition, Arnold announced that he would be retiring from professional bodybuilding. The astonished producer asked, *"So what's next for you?"* And Arnold's authentic and sincere response in his strongly accented English was: *"I have been the best bodybuilder in the world. Now I am going to Hollywood to be the best actor in the world."*

You can almost hear the chuckle coming from behind the camera and imagine the cameraman's thoughts: *Hollywood? You've got to be kidding. You have no formal education. You barely speak English, and people can't even pronounce your name. How are you going to make it in Hollywood?*

But the producers recognized something in Arnold Schwarzenegger immediately, and they decided to make him the star of the documentary. Arnold was genuine. He was sincere. He was authentic and personal. When speaking to the audience, he drew them in with his warmth, directness, and confidence. People come away liking the guy. Even before he became governor of California, Arnold Schwarzenegger had everyone's vote.

Whether you're a *Terminator* fan or not, take some lessons from Arnold and you'll be surprised at the powerful results they yield.

SUMMARY

The best communicators are adept at thinking on their feet. They are authentic, knowledgeable, and confident. Confidence builds credibility. Additionally, a speaker who conveys warmth and builds a connection with their audience will become likeable and gain support every time. The secret is to apply proven science to the delicate art of interpersonal communication.

MAKE IT REAL WORKSHEETS

What Does Excelling at Thinking on Your Feet Look Like?

We all have our heroes—people who always seem to know the right thing to say and appear to elevate their brand with every discussion, conversation, and presentation they make. Sometimes that very skill causes us to find them annoying or unlikeable, but more often than not, we are in awe. We want a little bit of what they have.

Let's deconstruct their magic. Breaking it down reduces most of the mystery. Identifying small, doable behaviors that make a big impact helps us see that excelling at thinking on your feet is actually not that hard to master.

A Speaking-On-Your-Feet Hero

Close your eyes. Imagine people you know at work, in your community, from college, casual friendships, respected colleagues, extended family members, and others. Who stands out in your mind as articulate, confident, and a speaking-on-your-feet hero?

Name one or more speaking-on-your-feet heroes.
When/where did you hear them speak that impressed you?

What was your overall impression of them and/or the situation?
What did they do well?
What characteristics did you see them exhibit that you most admired? Why?

No one is perfect.

What could they have done better?

____

____

____

How does being good at thinking on their feet benefit them in business and in life?

____

____

____

____

GEORGE GERSHWIN
American composer and pianist

Chapter 2

The Vital Signs: Pause! Then Apply CPR

So how do you demonstrate the power of thinking on your feet in those unexpected situations, hallway meetings, sudden phone calls, or other occasions when you have no time to prepare? You pause then gather your thoughts and come back with a smart and credible response!

EVERYONE IS WATCHING

When host Steve Harvey mistakenly declared the wrong contestant the winner of the 2015 Miss Universe Pageant, he turned a routine ceremony into one of the most cringeworthy moments in live television history. That was probably better proof than any of us needed that live speaking carries the potential for major mishaps.

To some extent, all conversations, all presentations that allow for audience interaction, and all communication events require some level of spontaneity and thinking on your feet. In Harvey's case, the authenticity of his response carried the moment.

"OK, folks, uh, there's—I have to apologize," Steve Harvey said moments after millions of Colombians had already started celebrating from their living rooms.

"The first runner-up is Colombia," he then clarified. *"Miss Universe 2015 is Philippines."*

DON'T MISS THE POINT

When I've mentioned to friends and colleagues that I'm writing a book about thinking on your feet and responding well in those difficult or awkward moments, a common response was: *"Yeah, you walk away thinking of what you could have said to put them in their place."* Or *"I wish I had the quick reaction to really give it to him and wipe that smirk off his face."* Or *"If only I had the nerve to tell them what I really thought."*

But they're missing the point. This book is not about getting the upper hand in a conflict or getting even. Thinking on your feet is not intended to win arguments, put the other person down, or come out on top. Quite the opposite.

A successful thinking-on-your-feet interaction should always be about extending the conversation, exploring other points of view, and finding understanding in order to identify the best solution possible at that moment in time.

> ***A successful thinking-on-your-feet interaction should always be about extending the conversation, exploring other points of view, and finding understanding.***

KNOW THE VITAL SIGNS

With this powerful idea in mind, I am introducing the Magic Formula for Thinking on Your Feet: Pause! Then apply CPR.

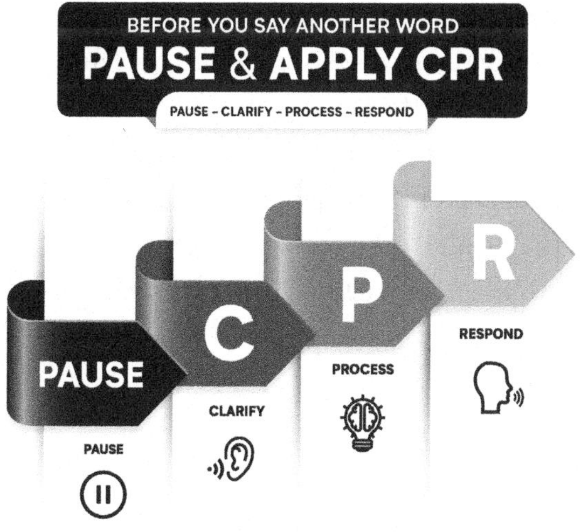

Pause!

Stop talking. Think. Listen.

When you're thrown that curveball, attacked with an insult, or just questioned unexpectedly, your heart races, your mouth dries, and your mind wants to react. Don't. This is when you need to do the most important thing . . . stop and pause . . . let silence fill the space. Take a moment to think and grasp the situation before you respond.

When you are caught off guard and thrown a curveball in a meeting or conversation, your emotional brain engages first. Stressed, you may tend to bypass rational thinking and react instinctively without giving yourself time to figure out what's really going on. In this situation, action/reaction occurs almost instantaneously.

The key to thinking on your feet is not to fall into the trap of reacting. Instead, you should pause. Take a breath, relax, and then use the CPR model to avoid being flustered or nervous, appearing incompetent, and even feeling that your heart is racing out of control. It's time to administer some CPR.

Then Apply CPR

Now that you have taken a deep breath, it's time to apply **CPR** to the situation. Bring back the life, energy, and positivity to the discussion. The CPR model is Clarify, Process, and Respond. Clarifying and processing before you respond (not react) will give you greater control in that heated or uncomfortable moment. It momentarily disengages your emotional brain and allows your thinking brain to take over.

Here's how:

C – Clarify

Inquire. Understand. Clarify the concern. Get to the core of the issue, the complaint, the comment, or the challenge. Understand the root of the question and the real concern behind the words. Ask the right questions, listen in the moment, and uncover the relevant details that will help you respond with intelligence, poise, and empathy.

P – Process

Once you understand the concern, the point of view, or the challenge being presented, you can begin to process and prepare your ideas for the reply. Make sense of the comment and combine it with your own information, logic, and experience. Be open to a new view. Trust your gut. Access your own depth of knowledge and experience. And put it all together for a clear, compelling, and organized response.

R – Respond

You clarified the question. You processed the information and organized your thoughts. Now it's time to respond with the confidence, poise, and agility that demonstrates your desire to be open, build a connection, gain trust, and move forward in the best way possible.

Every personal characteristic exhibited by those who are great at responding on their feet, as seen in the previous chapter, fits into one of the following *critical* steps.

Yes, critical! All four elements have to be applied to be successful at thinking on your feet.

If you don't **pause,** you are likely to react in the moment with negative consequences.

If you don't **clarify**, you may never understand the substance of the question.

If you don't **process** the information, you are likely to ramble, lose your train of thought, and watch your credibility evaporate.

And finally, if you don't **respond** with confidence, likeability, and poise, even the best response may not seem credible enough to satisfy your audience.

Like all communication, thinking on your feet is intended to build a relationship with your audience. It's not you vs. them . . . It's you *and* them to better understand each other and arrive at the best possible answer, resolution, or way forward.

Just when you feel that the situation is dire, Pause! Then apply CPR to rebuild the connection, extend the conversation, and bring renewed energy to the situation at hand.

SUMMARY

In challenging situations, there is nothing more powerful than the initial pause! It allows emotions to settle and realistic expectations to emerge. And once you've caught your breath, it's time to resuscitate the conversation by applying CPR!

CLARIFY the issue to ensure everyone is on the same page. Ask questions. Summarize with empathy and understanding.

PROCESS the information gathered, integrate your instinctive knowledge, and organize your thoughts for a strong and clear response.

RESPOND with confidence, likeability, and poise to build credibility and move the conversation forward in a positive way.

Don't skip a step! A successful thinking-on-your-feet interaction is about extending the conversation and being open to other points of view with the ultimate goal of arriving at the best solution possible.

MAKE IT REAL WORKSHEETS

Critical Elements for Thinking on Your Feet: Pause. Clarify. Process. Respond.

Every proficiency, every talent, is made up of fundamentals—basic rules and principles for success. Whether you're referring to football, medical treatments, legal procedures, architectural drawings, or thinking on your feet, every discipline starts with a formula.

The formula for successfully thinking on your feet requires the application of four critical elements, in their specific order and proficiency. Those elements are: pause, clarify, process, and respond. And yes, they are all critical to the process. If you don't **pause,** you are likely to react with negative consequences. If you don't **clarify**, you may never understand the question. If you don't **process** the information, you are likely to ramble. And finally, if you don't **respond** with confidence, even the best answer may not satisfy your audience.

Self-Analysis Is Always Healthy

Take a look at the fundamental process. Does it make sense? Do you buy it?

Buy-in is key to success. Think back to when you were playing sports and your team just didn't have the mojo, just wasn't in sync, or lacked luster. Your coach often said, "Let's get back to the fundamentals." And for some reason or other, that restart seemed to work. It put you back on track to achieving your goals.

That's why understanding and believing in the fundamentals is your key to victory. When you're a little off your game, simply refer back to the basics and it will get you back on track to where you want to go.

For you, what is the hardest element of thinking on your feet: pause, clarify, process, or respond? Why?

____

____

What is your technique for pausing? If you don't pause, why not? Do you think it's important?

___

___

___

How do you demonstrate active listening? What makes it difficult to clarify? What can you do to help with this challenge?

___

___

___

Do you take time to process the question and integrate the other person's ideas with your knowledge? What makes this difficult in the moment?

___

___

___

How do you typically respond? Are you defensive? Are you open to new ideas?

___

___

___

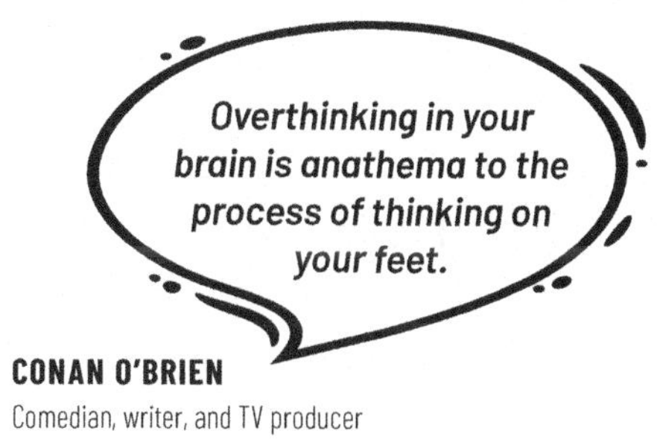

CONAN O'BRIEN
Comedian, writer, and TV producer

Chapter 3

Keep Calm and Carry On

Let's not ignore the possible elephant in the room. Many—if not most—people fear speaking in front of a group, large or small. In fact, the number-one greatest fear is public speaking. Death ranks at number six. Hmm... So is it preferable to be the one in the casket rather than the one giving the eulogy?

STOP SHAKING

Communicating your ideas and presenting them clearly is an essential component in all aspects of a successful life. Being a good public speaker can help you advance your career, grow your business, and form stronger relationships. It can help you promote ideas and move people to action. To do these things well requires a fair amount of standing in front of an audience and delivering a pitch, an idea, or a body of work. In no uncertain terms, it requires the ability to think on your feet with confidence, likeability, and poise. And sometimes, the only thing preventing you from a successful interaction is fear.

BE FEARLESS

We all want to be fearless speakers. We dream of confidently expressing our thoughts and calmly making our points while sounding honest, smart, and professional. But the reality is less than perfect. Too often, our fears take over and we imagine ourselves going blank, stumbling over words, forgetting our point, rambling on, and worst of all, embarrassing ourselves. And with every thought like this, our speaking anxiety spirals out of control.

If you fear public speaking, here's something to consider. Forbes business research shows that fear of public speaking has a 10 percent impairment on your wages and a 15 percent impairment on your promotion.

Fear of public speaking has a 10 percent impairment on your wages and a 15 percent impairment on your promotion.

And if that's not enough to motivate you to do something about it, here are five more reasons to focus on reducing your speaking anxiety from the book *Speaking Up without Freaking Out* by Dr. Matt Abrahams, professor of communication at Stanford University:

(1) Being nervous reduces your ability to think clearly, to make effective decisions, and to respond to your audience's reactions. In fact, people with high anxiety have a difficult time focusing, feed their own self-fulfilling prophecy, and truly become incoherent.

(2) People who appear nervous are often judged as being deceptive. Many behaviors associated with nervousness—avoiding eye contact, stumbling over words, pacing—are often linked to the perception of lying or hiding information. This means having anxiety about speaking can negatively influence how others see you. And when your trustworthiness is questioned, your ability to make an impact dramatically decreases.

(3) Anxiety is exhausting and thus affects mental processing, which often leads to either panicking and forgetting what you want to say or choking and overthinking to the point of rambling.

(4) Anxious speakers remember less. They remember fewer of their ideas and fewer details about those ideas. As a result, anxious speakers often struggle to think of the words and ideas they want to express. They end up saying, *"That didn't really come out the way I intended,"* or *"That's not what I meant to say."*

(5) Finally, being highly anxious about presenting affects your ability to evaluate your own speaking effectiveness. Not only does your anxiety negatively skew your ability to judge your own performance accurately, but your nervousness tends to make you misinterpret others' feedback as being more negative than it was intended.

Let's face it. It's nearly impossible to be an effective speaker if you don't get control over your anxiety. So do something about it!

Fear and anxiety aren't all bad news. In fact, they have some benefits. Your fear actually helps you focus your energy and provides you with motivation to work harder. So turn fear and anxiety on its head. Instead of letting the fear control you, it's time you took control of your fear.

Start with Something Easy

Take a deep breath.

There's a reason you've heard of this technique before. Because it works! More specifically, "belly breathing" slows you down by lowering your heart rate. Try it, right now. Place one hand on your upper chest and the other on your abdomen. Inhale slowly through your nose and fill your lower abdomen. Feel your lower hand expand with your abdomen while keeping your upper hand flat. Slowly release your breath through your nose and feel your abdomen contract. To occupy your mind, slowly count to four as you inhale and then again as you exhale. Focus your attention on the counting. Repeat this type of breathing several times. Notice your heart rate begin to slow and your body relax.

Keep Your Cool and Keep Your Power

Whether you're an athlete in an intense playoff game, a defendant on the stand in a contentious trial, or an employee delivering a presentation to senior management in an important meeting, you must be able to relax under pressure. If you get uptight under stressful situations, you're not alone. The fear of losing your cool is a real one; emotionally blowing up, becoming paralyzed, and freezing in the moment—or worse yet, bursting into tears—are all possibilities that will make you lose your power in front of others.

Your ability to stay calm is what allows you to think on your feet and make wise in-the-moment decisions. You can enhance your chances for a relaxed, confident, and poised interaction by using the following three techniques:

Be prepared – The better prepared you are, the more in control you will feel. Plan what you will say, build in stories and examples, anticipate questions that will be thrown at you, and prepare the answers. Know your opening, organize your content with a good structure, and plan your close.

Loosen your muscles – Olympic swimmers, ice skaters, and track runners loosen up before their events. They shake loose. Athletes know that when their bodies are relaxed, they will perform better. If you are able to master thinking on your feet, you will feel like you've won a gold medal. To do this, you will have to learn how to control your nerves, which in turn will give you greater presence of mind and emotion.

Before an important presentation or meeting, stand with your feet shoulder-width apart. Begin moving your fingers—just your fingers. Now add your hands and shake them too. One by one, add your elbows, shoulders, chest, waist, hips, knees, and feet until you're shaking all over. Let your head move with your body, shaking all the way down to your toes. Slowly come to a stop and let yourself settle then breathe easily and deeply down into your body.

Breathe deeply – As just stated, the most successful way to relax your body and focus your mind is simply to breathe. Taking deep breaths using your diaphragm is the oldest and still the best-known stress reducing technique. It has been used for centuries to quell anxiety and promote a general state of well-being.

Many people think that deep breathing means taking big gulps of air, but the word "deep" actually refers to the positioning in the body. Test yourself. Sit upright in a straight chair. Ask someone to stand behind you and lightly place his/her forearms on your shoulders so you feel the pressure but not pain. Take a big breath. If you feel an increased pressure of their arms on your shoulders, your breath is coming in too high. Take another breath, this time sending it deeper into your body so the pressure on your shoulders is reduced and you feel the expansion in the area around and just above your waist.

Be Mindful and Accept Your Emotions

Notice your feelings. Judge them. Name them. And admit your reactions. Take a moment to tell yourself, *This is me feeling nervous, angry, jealous, surprised.* And as you reflect, ask, *OK, now what do I do?* This technique encourages you to confront your feelings and ask yourself questions that help you move forward rather than letting the anxiety take over your reaction. Suddenly, your emotion fades a little as your logic steps in to manage your response. *Stop being so angry. It's not worth it. Calm down. Take control.*

This technique worked for me before I realized it was a technique. After completing my dissertation on "How to Create High-Performing Teams," I had to defend it to a group of professors, professionals, and fellow students. Here I was, surrounded by about forty-five colleagues, friends, and family. I was so nervous, my heart was pounding, my face was flushed, and my palms were sweaty. I could barely stand at the front of the classroom. When I shared my feelings with a friend, she wisely suggested that I actually tell the audience I am nervous, and this will help me move on. With little else to go on, I stepped up to the microphone and said, "Hi. I'm really nervous so please be patient." Everyone laughed and my anxiety level nearly disappeared completely. The best advice ever! Thank you, Ada.

IT TAKES COURAGE

Courage is not the absence of fear; it's the triumph over it.
—Nelson Mandela

According to Dr. Matt Abrahams, research has shown that acting courageous in the face of fear actually reduces the anxiety you feel.

For example, some research has demonstrated that introverts who initiate social interactions—even when it makes them feel uncomfortable or awkward—later report feeling better about themselves. And when verbally attacked or bullied, people lose their fear and become more courageous the more they push back on their provocateur.

As Ernest Hemingway put it: "Courage is grace under pressure." These techniques, some from Dr. Abraham's book, *Speaking*

Up without Freaking Out, will help build up your courage and instill grace and confidence in those fearsome situations.

Fight Your Negative Self-Talk

Most people spend a lot of time inside their own mind—worrying about the future, replaying events in the past, and focusing on a persistent negative dialog. They think:

I don't know enough about this topic.

I'm going to screw this up.

I should have prepared more.

Everyone can tell I'm nervous, and they think I'm unqualified.

They don't like me.

Unfortunately, these thoughts can often be persuasive and result in a self-fulfilling prophecy—you expect to do a poor job, so you do a poor job because you subconsciously made it happen.

The technique for reversing this vicious cycle is simply to replace negative comments with positive affirmation. Positive affirmations are simple messages. Repeated over and over, they begin to worm their way into your mind, slowly changing both your thinking and your reality.

Rather than saying, *"I'm going to mess this up,"* you instead say, *"This is a great opportunity to share my innovative ideas with my colleagues."* Note, this affirmation is not unbelievably positive. It's not saying, *"This is going to be the most incredible speech ever!"* It's just acknowledging the reality that you have good ideas; that makes you feel positive, which in turn makes you more relaxed. The more relaxed you are, the more likely you are to give a great presentation. You are creating a self-fulfilling prophecy to obtain a positive outcome, not a negative one.

You should think of some positive affirmations that are relevant and meaningful to you. Then, before you speak or present, you can consciously repeat one of these affirmations. Affirmations should not be long sayings or contain too many concepts. Athletes often use one-word mantras (e.g., focus, calm, fun) as they avoid overthinking the challenges of competing.

Here are some examples of positive affirmations:

- People will listen to my ideas with an open mind.
- The audience is interested in hearing my thoughts and ideas.
- I have something of value to share.
- I know this material well.
- My work will impact this discussion positively.
- I trust my experience and intuition.
- I have the smarts and ability to handle this.
- Focus.
- Calm.
- Fun.

A SIMPLE CONVERSATION

Many people see speaking as performing. When you are acting, you have exact lines to say and you are expected to act in a specific way. When an actor doesn't say their line at the right time or move to the right place on stage, it causes problems for the other actors and often creates confusion for the audience. In a performance, there is a right way and a wrong way. This performance anxiety is what causes many to get nervous, and for good reason: they worry they will do something wrong that will screw everything up.

But giving a speech or responding to a question in front of an audience is not a performance, and therefore, there is no right way or wrong way. Certainly, there are better ways, but there is no one perfect way. So, with that in mind, the nervous speaker must simply *reframe* the speaking situation as something *other* than a performance.

Research suggests that approaching presenting as a conversation rather than a performance can dramatically reduce anxiety and increase audience rapport. Most people who get nervous about giving a speech do not get nervous when having a conversation about the same topic with friends or coworkers. So, if you reframe the speaking situation as a conversation and not a performance, it will help you be less anxious and more comfortable.

SUMMARY

Being a good public speaker can help you advance your career, grow your business, and form strong relationships. But sometimes, the only thing that stands between you and your success is fear. So, instead of letting your fear of speaking control you, it's time you took control of your fear.

Confront your emotions and feel them lose their power. You are much stronger than you ever imagined and much smarter than you think.

MAKE IT REAL WORKSHEETS

Manage and Leverage Your Anxiety

It's nearly impossible to be an effective speaker if you don't get control of your anxiety. Why should you care? Well, if you don't become an effective speaker, Forbes suggests you are likely to be limiting both your promotional opportunities and your wages. And no one wants that!

And there are other practical reasons to control your fear. Nervousness reduces your ability to think clearly and respond to your audience's reaction. And then your audience whether wondering if you're being deceptive. Why else would you be so nervous?

Conquer your nervousness and you are well on your way to being a confident, thoughtful, and smart conversationalist.

Your Anxiety, Your Way

We each react to anxiety differently. Some talk fast; others fidget or pace. As a start, be mindful of your behavior so you can control it.

List the small, subtle, obvious behaviors you demonstrate when you're anxious in the moment.

____

____

____

What techniques can you use to combat your nervous behaviors?

How can you apply these techniques next time you notice your anxious behavior appearing?

____

____

____

Positive Speak

Don't be your own worst enemy with persistent negative dialog, lack of confidence, and harmful self-talk.

Write down three to five positive affirmations you can use that specifically challenge your own negative self-talk. Make them simple and straightforward concepts, easy to remember and repeat.

____

____

____

Make It a Conversation

Research shows that a little anxiety is healthy; it gets your adrenalin pumping, gives you energy, and forces you to focus. That's good news, since it's unlikely all your anxiety will ever disappear in critical situations.

To manage your anxiety, reframe the situation. Instead of a performance, tell yourself you are simply having a conversation about a specific topic. Conversations don't have to be perfect; they simply have to be natural.

Identify a person in your life with whom you are most comfortable having a conversation, whether it revolves around different points of view, explaining something in detail, or simply sharing an idea. Then bring this person to mind next time you are caught in a thinking-on-your-feet moment and need to reframe your delivery into a conversation.

Identify one, two, or three people you can bring to mind in a difficult thinking-on-your-feet moment to help you turn a lecture into a conversation.

Who are they and what makes them easy to talk to?

____

____

____

PART
2
Pause!
Then Apply CPR

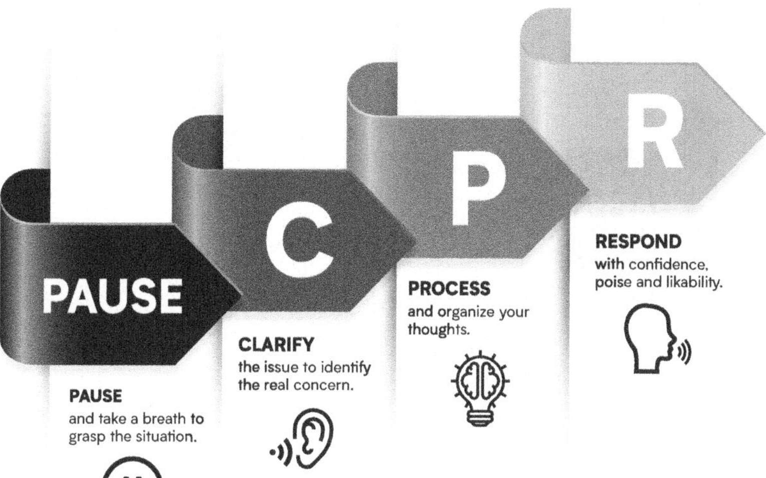
BEFORE YOU SAY ANOTHER WORD
PAUSE & APPLY CPR
PAUSE – CLARIFY – PROCESS – RESPOND
PAUSE
C
P
R
PAUSE
and take a breath to grasp the situation.
CLARIFY
the issue to identify the real concern.
PROCESS
and organize your thoughts.
RESPOND
with confidence, poise and likability.

BEFORE YOU SAY ANOTHER WORD
PAUSE & APPLY CPR
PAUSE – CLARIFY – PROCESS – RESPOND
PAUSE
C
CLARIFY
P
PROCESS
R
RESPOND
PAUSE
and stop to take a breath. Grasp the situation & let silence fill the air.

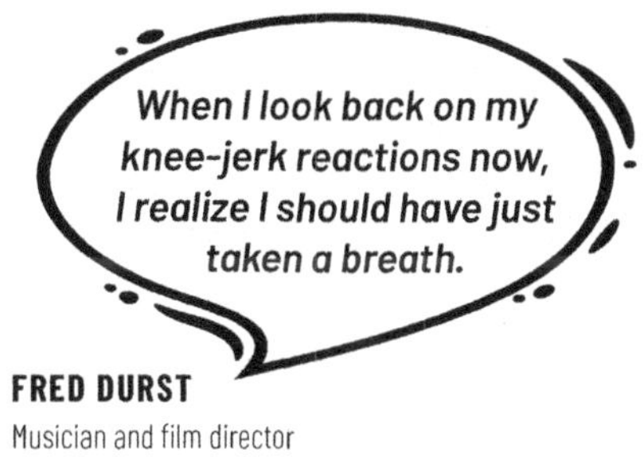

FRED DURST
Musician and film director

Chapter 4

Pause!

When you're caught off guard with a question or comment that may not sit comfortably with you, your heart races, your face gets flushed, and all too quickly—you react. Don't!

Stop. Pause. Control the impulse of your subconscious mind. Take a minute to collect your thoughts.

DON'T REACT. RESPOND.

A reaction is a reflex. It's driven by personal principles, biases, and preconceptions of the unconscious mind—the part of your brain that takes no time to think or evaluate the situation. It's a reaction to the moment, usually connected to the past, that doesn't take into consideration long-term effects or consequences of the behavior. It's a survival technique, a defense mechanism that helps you cope in the moment but is often regretted later.

A response, however, comes more slowly. It's based on information from both the conscious mind and the subconscious mind. A response takes into consideration the many factors surrounding the situation.

A reaction and a response may look alike. But they're very different.

Reactions are the result of underlying assumptions and beliefs that may not have been thought through. And the results might be anything from embarrassing to catastrophic. Reacting is giving away power. Responding is keeping power.

Pause before you speak, and you will keep the power as you respond with confidence and poise.

The Power of the Pause

Excellent speakers are masters of the pause. They are comfortable with silences. They take a breath, relax, and smile before speaking. They know that the pause is a key part of communication.

Pauses are both powerful and necessary in every speaking situation. Powerful because they show strength on the part of the speaker. The speaker has the confidence to let their words, or silence, stand for some length of time, rather than filling in the moments compulsively with sounds. And necessary simply because the listener also needs time to hear what's been said, reflect on it, and file it away.

The speaker has the confidence to let their words, or silence, stand for some length of time.

BEFORE YOU SAY ANOTHER WORD . . . PAUSE!

When you're confronted, caught off guard, momentarily stunned, or simply trying to influence someone else's thinking . . . this is when you must pause. This is the most important pause of all.

Stop. Pause. Take a breath. And use this time to think.

These are the seconds that will manage your emotions, frame your response, and determine the success of the interaction. If you learn any lesson from Steve Jobs (or this book), it is to pause before you say another word.

Pauses let your mind stay ahead of your mouth. As the speaker, you are performing several tasks simultaneously. The first is ensuring you understand the comment or question, then thinking about what you will say when you respond, and finally, projecting your words in a clear, concise, and effective interaction with the other person.

Ideally, you're in the moment listening and accessing your internal information and ideas for a response. Pausing gives you the advantage of letting your quick-thinking and active mind get ahead of your mouth so your words are thoughtful and more meaningful to the listener.

For most people, the simple act of pausing is really hard. How do you stop, breathe, and think in the moment—when your mind is racing, your heart is pounding, and your instincts want to react? But this is important. This is what separates the excellent communicators and leaders from the rest of the pack. This is your challenge.

Your Personal Pause Cue

Everyone is different. Coping methods are unique. So you must come up with a "pause cue" that works for you, that stops you in your tracks to remind you to apply the most important pause of all—the one you use before you say another word. My close friend and colleague Joshua has mastered controlling his pause. At a recent client meeting where the data in his presentation was questioned, his reaction was powerful. He looked at the client, smiled, picked up a pen, and said, "Interesting." One word. That was his pause. That gave him the time he needed to collect himself and respond calmly and professionally to the client.

Joshua's pause cue is to smile and then look for something to pick up—a piece of paper or a pencil, cup, or water bottle—any object that allows him to be momentarily distracted so he can make that important pause.

Communications expert Marian Woodall suggests that a few extra seconds can be gained by a nonverbal gesture. This indicates you've heard the question and you're preparing a response with a nod, a slight lift of the hand, or a smile (but never a grimace). People who ask difficult questions usually know they are doing so and will appreciate your thoughtfulness in a measured response. If you begin to speak the instant the questioner closes their mouth, you may sound as if you have a canned answer ready to pull out. People feel they deserve a personal response. Taking time to think is seen as a compliment; you are saying—nonverbally—*I think your question is a good one, and I'm going to give you a well-thought-out response.*

Come up with a "pause cue" that works for you—that stops you in your tracks.

One Small Pause, So Many Uses

Keep in mind that your speech or your response is not a monologue. A conversation is a dialogue between your words and your listener's thoughts. Pauses allow your audience to digest and mentally interact with your words. A skilled speaker will often engage their audience more with their pauses than with their speaking.

Taking time to think is seen as a compliment.

Inspirational speaker Kwesi Millington suggests these powerful ways to use pauses in your response:

A skilled speaker will often engage their audience more with their pauses than with their speaking.

Pause in transition. When you are making several points or offering different perspectives, pausing between ideas lets the audience reflect on what you're saying while helping them keep pace with your own thinking. So pause between words or let silence fill your movement on stage.

Pause for drama. Sometimes a little theatrics goes a long way. If you are building momentum for an idea or story and finally reaching the most salient point, moral conclusion, or simple truth, a dramatic pause punctuates those important words, ensuring your audience is listening and waiting to hear what's coming next. President John F. Kennedy famously paused and said, *"Ask not what your country can do for you . . . (pause, pause) . . . Ask what you can do for your country."* Pausing both before and during this powerful quote, JFK impacted his audience with silence and allowed his listeners to grasp the very big idea behind his words.

Pause for reflection. Give your audience time to reflect on a concept or a question. Encourage your listeners to think and come to their own conclusions with the reflective pause. Whether asking a rhetorical question, presenting a new idea, or simply challenging common beliefs, the reflective pause brings your audience in and makes them part of your presentation. *"Think for a moment about how you would feel if _______?"* Pause. Give the audience time to reflect. This encourages the audience's ideas to be a part of your presentation.

Pause for the senses. Use this to support a description that appeals to the senses. For example, *"A beautiful summer afternoon . . . (pause) . . . imagine it . . . (pause) . . . willows softly rustling in* *the warm breeze. . .(pause). . .birds chirping in trees. . .(pause) sitting with a cool glass of lemonade in your hand . . ."* Create a heightened feeling within the mind of your audience by pausing to allow their senses to take hold.

Pause for the unexpected. There will be times when the situation or the audience is not in your control. A loud truck might be passing your window, a group in the audience may be talking loudly among themselves, a cell phone might ring, etc. Don't compete with the audience or those distractions. Pause and wait. You might even interact to make the moment light: *"Is that for me?"* (when the cell phone rings), or *"Sounds like you're discussing an important idea. Are you willing to share?"* (when there is a side conversation), or simply wait for the distraction to pass and then continue.

Pause at the start and at the end. Pause to take in the audience before you begin to speak, whether you are just starting your presentation or responding to a question. And like bookends, pause when you have finished with your comments. Let your final words make a lasting impression. Pause when you are done responding, before continuing with your presentation, and before you leave the stage. Remember, pause has power.

Pauses are an important part of any interaction. The effective use of conversational and speech pauses is a technique to be mastered.

SUMMARY

Pauses are both powerful and necessary in every speaking situation. Powerful because they show strength on the part of the speaker and necessary because the listener also needs time to hear what's been said. Be sure to come up with your own personal pause cue that helps you close your mouth when your first instinct is to speak.

Pauses are a communication technique worthy of mastering. Pause for transition or to build drama when making a key point. You might pause to allow your audience to reflect on a new idea or be surprised by an unexpected conclusion. The silent pause has the power to shift the conversation. Use it wisely.

MAKE IT REAL WORKSHEETS

Shhhhhhh. Stop. Your boss asks a tricky question. Your team requests a quick update. The CEO wants to understand why you chose to go down this path. Your heart starts to pound. Your mind is racing. Your palms are sweating. But don't say another word. Pause!

Fight or flight kicks in. Since it seems unprofessional or unfriendly to flee the scene, our instinct is often to fight, to react in the moment, to make it a me vs. them clash.

When you react in the moment, you give up your power. When you pause and take time to think, you harness the power of the moment and collect yourself for a better response.

The Power of the Pause! Pauses are powerful and necessary. Powerful because they show strength and confidence on behalf of the speaker. Necessary because they let the mouth catch up with your mind.

Imagine being confronted with a question or comment that catches you off guard. What personal tip or trick . . . your own *personal pause cue*, can you apply to help you pause, stop, and reflect in the moment, before you respond?

____

____

____

Pauses have the ability to bring power to your words, expand on your thoughts, and help the listener hear between the lines.

How would you use pauses to make these dialogues stronger? Read each aloud. Then read through again, using a colored pen to insert a slash mark (/) where you might pause. If you think a longer pause would make it even more effective, use several slash marks. Now read the dialog aloud again, pausing with your marks and noting the difference. On a scale of 1 to 10, how much more powerful is the dialogue with the appropriate pauses?

Movie: ***Wall Street*** Dialogue: **Gordon Gekko is explaining "Greed is good."**
POST PAUSE SCORE (1-10): _____

"The point is ladies and gentleman that greed for lack of a better word is good. Greed is right greed works. Greed clarifies cuts through and captures the essence of the evolutionary spirit. Greed in all of its forms greed for life for money for love knowledge has marked the upward surge of mankind. And greed you mark my words will not only save Teldar Paper but that other malfunctioning corporation called the USA. Thank you very much."

Movie: ***Any Given Sunday*** Dialogue: **Al Pacino's pregame speech**

POST PAUSE SCORE (1-10): _____

"I don't know what to say really. Three minutes to the biggest battle of our professional lives all comes down to today. Now either we heal as a team or we're gonna crumble. Inch by inch, play by play—till we're finished. We're in hell right now gentleman. Believe me. And we can stay here get the shit kicked out of us or we can fight our way back into the light. We can climb out of hell one inch at a time. Now I can't do it for you I'm too old. I look around I see these young faces and I think I mean I made every wrong choice a middle-aged man can make. I uh I pissed away all my money believe it or not I chased off anyone who's ever loved me and lately I can't even stand the face I see in the mirror."

Speech: **Naval Adm. William H. McRaven, University of Texas Commencement on May 17, 2014**

POST PAUSE SCORE (1-10): _____

"The university's slogan is 'What starts here changes the world.' I have to admit I kinda like it. 'What starts here changes the world.' Tonight there are almost eight thousand students graduating from UT. That great paragon of analytical rigor Ask.Com says that the average American will meet ten thousand people in their lifetime. That's a lot of folks but if every one of you changed the lives of just ten people and each one of those folks changed the lives of another ten people—just ten—then in five generations 125 years the class of 2014 will have changed the lives of eight hundred million people. Eight hundred million people think of it—over twice the population of the United States. Go one more generation and you can change the entire population of the world: eight billion people."

BEFORE YOU SAY ANOTHER WORD

PAUSE & APPLY CPR

PAUSE – CLARIFY – PROCESS – RESPOND

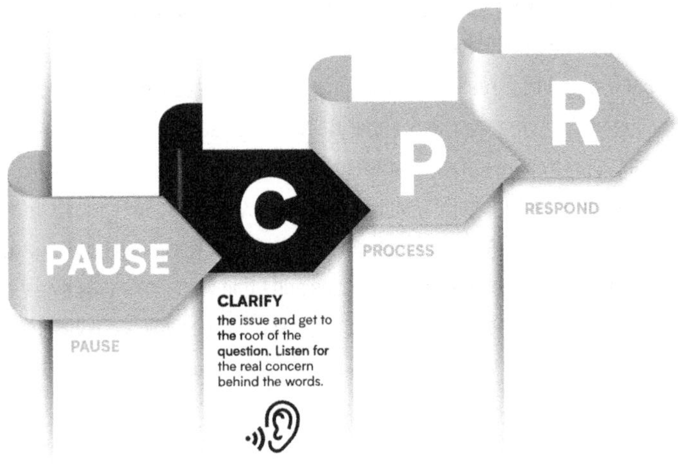

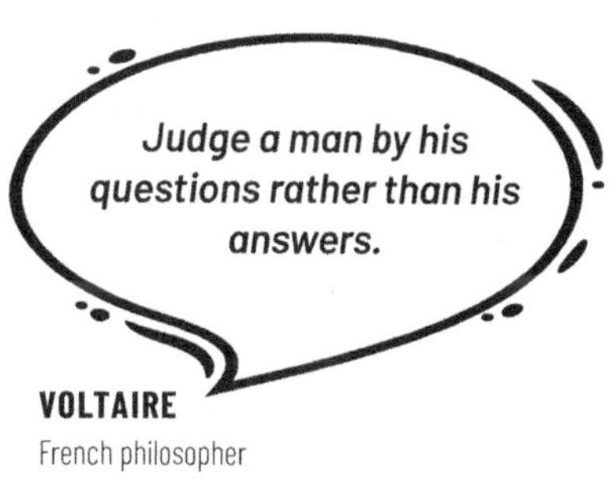

VOLTAIRE
French philosopher

Chapter 5
Clarify

A hand is raised. The audience looks. Will you answer a question? Will you consider a comment, another point of view? All this is a reflection of your ability to build trust, instill confidence, and influence your audience.

When people ask questions, often they are not simply looking for an answer to their query. What they really want to know is: Are you reliable? Can you be trusted? Are you in charge here? Do you know what you're talking about? Will my commitment, or trust, or money, or kids . . . be safe with you?

CLARIFY

"Thank you. I'd love to hear your question or comment."
"Thank you. That's a great question!"
"I'm glad you brought that up."

And now it's time for you to really start thinking on your feet.

Listen. Clarify. Hear the tone. Ensure you understand exactly what is being asked, said, or suggested. Question, clarify, and gather the facts before you respond.

It's good news when someone raises their hand, asks a question, and engages in the conversation.

Remind yourself that it's good news when someone raises their hand, asks a question, and engages in the conversation. They are interested in the topic. They want to talk about it, share their perspective, add value to the conversation. This is your opportunity to shine.

Conquer the Tough Questions

Often a question seems unanswerable because it's long, winding, complicated, multifaceted, or obscure. It's probably not intended to stump you. Perhaps the questioner simply hasn't thought out the question well enough in advance and the result is a vague question. Don't try to answer an unclear question, because you likely won't find a pleasing answer. You need to explore further.

Sometimes the questioner doesn't know enough about the topic to phrase the question well. So, help them. Ask thoughtful, open-ended questions to get to the root of their inquiry or concern. As hard as it may seem, try—or at least attempt—to understand where their thoughts are coming from. Empathize.

Other times the questioner with lots on his or her mind tries to get it all into one query; the result is a rambling question with many aspects. Don't try to answer it all or figure out what part of that question is most important. Ask for clarification.

But every so often, the questioner is trying to stump you, either because he has it in for you or he just wants to show off. People who deliberately ask difficult questions believe that a complicated question will pin you right to the wall. Don't let that happen.

Here are powerful techniques to explore further, identify the root of the inquiry, get clarification, and simplify complicated questions.

Can You Repeat That?

If a query appears difficult or confusing, ask for the question to be repeated. When you ask someone to repeat their question, they have a chance to review it themselves. Often, they are glad to repeat it, to have another chance to sound more knowledgeable and less confused. They might begin with: *"What I was trying to say was . . ."* The second time, the question will likely be shorter, more specific, and more focused. The query goes from confusing to straightforward. Repeating the question also buys you a few valuable seconds to process your response.

Rephrase and Restate

If the questioner seems unsure of the direction to take their comment, you have the opportunity to bring the topic back to your agenda by rephrasing the question. This also allows you to neutralize a negative approach and put a positive spin on the comment.

EXAMPLE:

Audience member: "Have you thought about the impact on our customers?"
Your rephrase: "Sounds like you're asking if I have considered the personal impact on our customers to ensure they have a positive experience during the product upgrade."

Narrow the Focus

If a question is so broad it would require an entire presentation to answer all aspects, ask a question of your own to both clarify the query and bring the discussion down to a manageable scope.

EXAMPLE:

"You're interested in hearing how I've considered the impact on our clients? What impacts are you more interested in, customer service or cost?"

Ask for Amplification

You are attempting to uncover what the speaker wants to know and demonstrating your interest in understanding their perspective. Do not lose sight of the fact that your goal is more than just giving information; it is successful communication with another person. There is no point in responding with information the seeker is not seeking.

> **EXAMPLE:**
> "When you say you want to know how I've analyzed the impact on our clients, do you mean you want a detailed analysis or a description of the tools and methods I used?"

Get a Definition

Jargon or terminology may present a problem. Be confident enough to ask that a specific term or acronym to be defined. Saying *"I'm not familiar with that term"* shows confidence. This is not a sign of ignorance. It's purely a clarification. It's also not uncommon for words to have more than one interpretation. Be sure you are all using those words with the same meaning.

> **EXAMPLE:**
> "Could you clarify what you mean by excess?" or "Process improvement is a complicated subject. Can you be more specific?"

No point in trying to respond intelligently when the answer will not satisfy the question.

Your co-worker might ask for a fast turnaround on a project. What is fast to them may not be fast to others. Do they mean a one-hour, one-day, or one-week turnaround? These vague words can be confusing, and assumptions need to be clarified. It is not necessary for you to agree with the definition, just to understand how the questioner is using the word.

Here are other examples of vague words and assumptions:

- Complete analysis
- Turnkey
- Easy/simple
- Value-added
- Quick turnaround
- Rigorous
- Analysis
- Moral
- Available resources
- Economic influence
- Competitive impact
- ASAP

Habit 5: Seek first to understand then to be understood.
—Stephen Covey, *The 7 Habits of Highly Successful People*

The wisdom of Stephen Covey has survived decades because of its simple truth. Covey suggests that most people seek to immediately get their perspective across, to be heard and acknowledged. Often, the result is lack of understanding, neglecting the key message, or missing the point entirely. Instead of listening to understand, many are simply waiting their turn to reply. Rather than being in the moment, the mind is filtering through comments and statements that will reinforce their own thinking. The result is classic miscommunication with a negative outcome.

To quote Yogi Berra, "You can hear a lot just by listening." Listening in the moment is the best way to truly understand another person's question, comment, viewpoint, idea, or challenge. And before you take the bold step of responding, especially in front of an audience or group, be sure you understand the question.

> ***Yogi Berra said, "You can hear a lot just by listening."***

Only by fully understanding the question or comment can the speaker respond successfully. A successful response is confident, informative, clear, and succinct.

To listen in the moment is to "actively" listen. That means putting all your own thoughts aside while focusing on the words, tone, body language, and emotion of the person speaking to you. Don't plan what you will say. Never get angry or defensive. Simply listen to their perspectives with empathy and understanding.

This is not easy. We often react and instantly get into fight mode—defending our idea and trying desperately not to lose. Fact is, real professionals—those who are knowledgeable, confident, and open to finding the best solution—don't fight; they listen. The most effective professionals are interested in the other perspective. You must actively listen if you want to be successful thinking on your feet.

LISTEN, LISTEN, AND THEN LISTEN SOME MORE

Actively Listen

Active listening involves listening with all senses: reading between the lines, being sensitive to tone, using eye contact to connect, and paying close attention to body language. Being an objective observer and seeing someone who is trying their best to share an idea or simply be heard can be a virtue.

Active listeners listen with empathy. They put themselves in the mindset and perspective of the speaker, just for the moment, in order to fully understand their viewpoint. Empathy has its own power. If others believe you understand them, they will try to understand you.

Listening Is Hard

People are listening all the time. We listen to gather information, to understand, to learn, and to enjoy. You'd think we'd be good at it. But it turns out, even with a lifetime of experience, people remember less than half of what they hear, according to Edgar Dale's book *Cone of Experience*. The reason is that our mind is racing, planning our response, defending our point of view.

Active listening is when you make a conscious effort to understand others so you get their complete message from their point of view and with good intention. First, you need to pay attention. This seems obvious, but since it's the key element, it's worth mentioning. Make eye contact with the person talking to you. Ignore outside noises, others' voices, and interruptions. Most importantly, put aside your own thoughts and resist the urge to plan your response with each point made.

Let the other person see you listen by nodding your head, smiling, occasionally confirming with a "yes." All these actions signal to the person that you respect their viewpoint and are open to their perspective.

When thinking on your feet in front of an audience or in a one-on-one interaction, actively listening is at the root of understanding and sets the stage for your response. Here's how:

Quiet

Stop talking; start listening. Keep your reaction in check until you gather the facts and plan your response.

Observe Body Language for Silent Clues

Is this a question or an accusation? Most people are simply trying to understand and make new information compatible within their own thinking.

Be in the Moment

Silence the mind chatter. Don't jump to conclusions or prepare your response. Focus on the speaker.

Picture What They're Saying

Make an effort to understand them even if you don't agree. Listen with empathy and try understanding their point of view.

Keep an Open Mind

There might be other right answers. Yes, you have your opinion, but be willing to be open to others and willing to change it.

Explore to Understand

At this point, you should have a good understanding of the question or comment. But this doesn't mean you have enough information to intelligently and confidently respond.

Before moving forward, dig a little deeper. Consider engaging in a brief conversation by asking questions that will get to the heart of the matter. Questions are the key to unlocking doors, providing insight, and bridging the gap of understanding. They are the fuel to a healthy and productive conversation.

Executives and other professionals have shared this list of questions they ask when engaged in a conversation that requires quick thinking and a smart response:

Consider engaging in a brief conversation by asking questions that will get to the heart of the matter.

1. Can you give an example?
2. Why do you believe that to be the case?
3. What is your top concern?
4. What specific feedback have you gotten?
5. What is the worst-case scenario? If the worst happens, how would you handle it?
6. Do you have a suggestion for a better result?
7. What outcome would be ideal?
8. What has worked well for you before that we might apply here?
9. What is the most challenging part of this recommendation for you?
10. What obstacles are getting in the way of success?

Feel free to add questions that are right for your situation. Then highlight, write down, and practice those questions that would help you listen in preparation for thinking on your feet and responding effectively next time.

SUMMARY

When people ask questions, they're not just looking for an answer; they are using the conversation as an opportunity to gain better insight into you. They want to see how you handle the interaction, pull your thoughts together, and articulate your response. Use it as an opportunity to shine.

Set yourself up for success. Don't attempt to answer a question until you're sure what is being asked. It's up to you to clarify, uncover the relevant facts, identify the emotion and meaning behind the comment, and narrow the focus in preparation of your response. Never be defensive. Use positive questioning techniques to build a connection as you reveal the concern.

MAKE IT REAL WORKSHEETS

You Can't Respond Until You Understand the Question

Great news! They're really listening and interested enough to ask a question. Now all you have to do is understand what they're asking so you can respond, right? Sounds simple enough.

The only problem is sometimes the questions aren't very clear. Perhaps the inquiry is taking you off on a tangent or appears to incorporate details not relevant to the discussion. This is your opportunity to pull it all together, dig in, clarify, and create a shared understanding.

Rephrase. Take the opportunity to rephrase the question for clarification and alignment with your agenda.

For example: In a discussion about the budget for the new product packaging, the question is asked: "Have you explored other options?" As this question is quite broad, it has the potential to veer the discussion off track. In this case, you might rephrase the question to realign with the topic in this way: "Are you asking if we explored less costly options?"

Rephrase: Imagine you are speaking about improving the productivity of the customer service team. How might you rephrase this question?

Question: How do you think the customer service reps will respond to the more complicated data gathering process?

Rephrase question to align with topic:

____

____

____

____

____

Rephrase: Imagine you are presenting the marketing programs planned for the next quarter. How might you rephrase this question?

Question: What product features do our customers want?

Rephrase question to align with topic:

____

____

____

____

____

____

Narrow the focus. Responses are much more likely to be successful when they answer the very specific question or issue at hand. Help yourself and your listener by narrowing the focus of the query so that a precise answer is likely.

For example, when asked, "What are the plans for the conference?" you might narrow the focus with a response such as, "Are you asking about the conference theme or the location and logistics?"

Narrow the focus: Imagine speaking about the architectural plans for the new building. How might you narrow the focus?

Question: How will the open spaces be developed?

Narrow the focus of the question:

____

____

____

____

____

____

Ask for a definition. This helps put everyone on the same page. Some words mean different things to different people. I might consider 12:05 on time for a noon meeting, while others might consider 11:59 the time people should arrive. When a comment leaves room for interpretation, it's good to clarify the meaning.

For example, when asked, "Did you do a rigorous analysis of the survey responses before you committed to this design?" you might clarify by asking, "Do you mean did I personally review all the responses?"

Ask for a definition: Imagine speaking about the upcoming fundraising campaign. How might you get a better definition?

Question: Is the online fundraising platform easier to use?

Ask for definition:

____

____

____

____

____

____

____

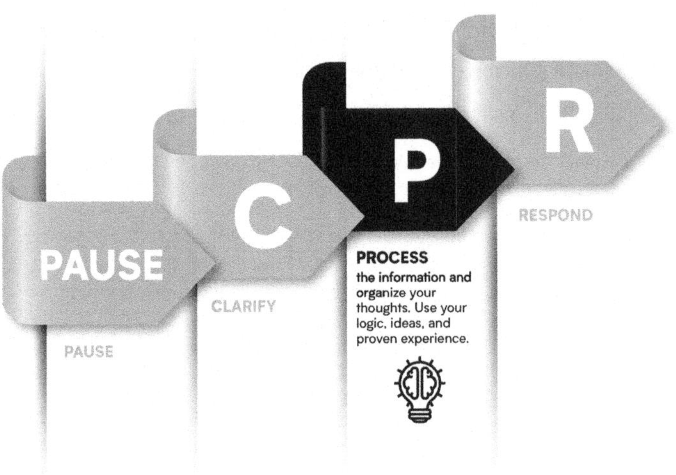
BEFORE YOU SAY ANOTHER WORD
PAUSE & APPLY CPR
PAUSE - CLARIFY - PROCESS - RESPOND
PAUSE
C
P
R
PAUSE
CLARIFY
PROCESS
the information and organize your thoughts. Use your logic, ideas, and proven experience.
RESPOND

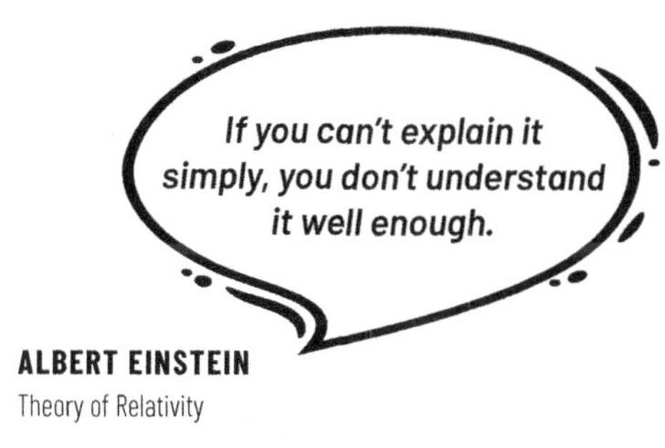

ALBERT EINSTEIN
Theory of Relativity

Chapter 6
Process

We've paused then clarified to uncover the valid viewpoints, challenges, and facts behind the query or comment.

Now it's time to process and develop a coherent response to the question asked using relevant information and personal experience in a logical, understandable way. The goal is to simply respond in a clear, confident, and compelling way that builds trust and promotes understanding. Fortunately, it's a lot easier than it sounds.

The goal is to simply respond in a clear, confident, and compelling way that builds trust and promotes understanding.

LOGIC VS. INTUITION

When thinking on your feet, you are working with your whole brain by integrating the logical left side of your brain with the intuitive right side. Rational thought and emotional thought occur in two different sides of the brain. Of course, it's all one brain, but it can be helpful for our purposes to suspend reason and imagine you actually have two brains.

The left brain is the logic brain that thinks. It provides you with the ability to ponder, reflect, consider, contemplate, decide, and interpret. The left side is known to be analytical, linear, sequential, verbal, concrete, rational, goal-oriented, and explicit.

The right brain is the emotional brain that feels and is intuitive. It tells you what you like and don't like, what pleases you, what thrills you, what causes you anguish, and what you fear. The right side is known to be spontaneous, visual, emotional, physical, symbolic, diffuse, nonverbal, and artistic.

Successfully thinking on your feet happens when your logical left brain and your intuitive right brain work in concert to help you through the interaction. When the left brain and the right brain work in harmony with each other, they help you to navigate through difficult conversation, to effectively respond to curveballs, to overcome being emotionally hijacked, and to confidently address challenging questions. The magic of this perfect partnership that leads to thinking on your feet is called structure spontaneity.

STRUCTURE IS THE KEY TO SUCCESS

Giving structure to your thoughts provides clarity and simplicity. Without it, you are likely to ramble on and make no point at all. Structure will shape your content in a logical, organized, and relevant way.

When your thought-out presentation is interrupted with a curveball question, your mind is in overdrive, working to make sense of the new input while accessing information from your own data bank to incorporate into a persuasive response. It's time to get your mind organized. Pull together all your information so it makes sense to you first. If you don't know what you're talking about, neither will anyone else.

Let go of the long-winded stories, irrelevant facts, general grievances, and useless information cluttering your mind. Focus on what's important. Use the facts collected and combine them with your own knowledge and gut response. More often than not, it's about less rather than more. Don't try to cram every little detail into your response—operate on a desire-to-know basis. If they ask, you can supply more information. If your response is adequate, stop talking.

In order for you to come across as knowledgeable, you've got to present your ideas in a logical way so the listener not only understands what you're saying but believes you know what you're talking about. A logical and organized response gives you authority and builds credibility.

Have a Plan

The fact is, in order to be successful at work or in life, you had better have a plan. This applies to all areas of life, from the story below about robbing a casino to professionally thinking on your feet.

Dapper Danny Ocean, the lead character in the movie *Ocean's Eleven*, is a man with a very big plan. Less than twenty-four hours into his parole from a New Jersey penitentiary, the charismatic thief is already rolling out his next plan. In one night, Danny and his ten-man crew of specialists steal over $150 million from three Las Vegas casinos owned by a ruthless entrepreneur who happens to be dating Danny's ex-wife. The entire movie focuses on Danny's elaborate plan and orchestrating it to perfection—pulling off the most daring heist in the history of Las Vegas. It's not easy. The plan requires pickpocketing, demolition, technology mastery, and daring acrobatics. But solid planning pays off as the team rides away with the $150 million. And if that weren't enough, Danny even gets the girl in the end. Amazing what a good plan (and a nice Hollywood budget) will get you.

Most plans are not as elaborate, don't require such a diverse set of skills, and don't result in a $150 million payout. But all successful efforts require a plan. Even thinking on your feet.

Create a structure and plan your response, and your chances of success will skyrocket.

Trust Your Gut and Focus on the Goal

Trust what you know. Use your intellect to maximize your understanding and come up with an impressive response.

This is the time to focus on what's important. Don't lose track of the purpose of this interaction or conversation. If your goal is to move a project along, be sure your response leads to a next step. If your goal is to gain additional funding or resources for your team, be sure to link your response in a way that will move the conversation in that direction. Never lose track of your desired end result or outcome.

Don't let comments and questions distract you from the purpose of the conversation unless you uncover information that negates your ability to move in your intended direction. Remember, your objective is always to arrive at the best possible outcome. If this means your initial recommendation or desired outcome no longer makes sense, then be open to abandoning your initial thoughts and pivot as required.

In his book *Think on Your Feet—Techniques to Analyze, Organize and Present Ideas Persuasively*, Dr. Keith Spicer points out that your aim is to organize your thoughts for clarity, brevity, and impact.

Clarity. Your response should be clear in both theme and construction. You've got to decide on your main point and tie your comments and examples to your central theme. Keep it simple.

It's a good idea to connect the questioner's comments and wording directly to your response. When you use their words and concepts, it shows you are truly listening. This builds trust and helps get buy-in even from the biggest skeptics.

Brevity. Getting to the point with key arguments makes a strong impression. Too much information is confusing and may leave room for nit-picking. If few words get the point across, your response will be that much more convincing.

Impact. To persuade the audience, you must make an impact—move them intellectually or emotionally. You make a powerful impact when you carry the audience with your story, logic, and flow. This is at the root of persuasion. Capture their minds with logic and carry their hearts with your rhythm and flow.

THE POWERFUL RULE OF THREE

Using the Rule of Three allows you to express concepts simply, emphasizing your points and increasing the memorability of your message. Quite simply, threes give structure to your thoughts.

"That's the truth, the whole truth, and nothing but the truth."

Examples of threes show up everywhere in our society: movies, history, business, and books:

- *The Good, the Bad and the Ugly*
- Superman's creed: Truth, justice, and the American way
- US Declaration of Independence: Life, Liberty and the pursuit of Happiness
- Three keys to real estate: location, location, location
- *The Three Musketeers*

- *The Three Little Pigs*
- Rock, paper, scissors
- Body, mind, and spirit
- Blood, Sweat & Tears
- On your mark, get set, go!

The secret to effective communication is the Rule of Three. We find things easier to follow when we can break it down to remember three key things.

In his book, *Brief: Make a Bigger Impact by Saying Less,* Joseph McCormack explains that the Rule of Three allows you to simplify information, provide balance, and keep people engaged. Here are three reasons why it works:

1. **Threes establish logic and simplicity**. It makes it easier for both you and the audience to stay on track.
2. **Threes provide balance and order**. There is a clear expectation of how long they need to listen and how you are progressing.
3. **Threes keep them connected**. The audience stays engaged because they know where they are, like chapters in a book.

When you *flag* your message by calling out the number of key ideas you want to share, says McCormick, people pay attention. When you say: *"I made that decision for three reasons . . ."* or *"This proposal will benefit your team in three ways . . ."* or *"The three most important things to remember are . . ."* then people pay attention. It signals that an organized and logical message is coming.

Simply put, chunking your response into three of something helps the listener track your thoughts while you sound smart and organized.

SIMPLE STRUCTURE

The key to successful speaking, whether it be spontaneous or planned, is to have structure. This helps you guide your audience from their initial question to where you want them to go with your response. Structure leads to clarity.

Clarity means being understood. While 100000000 is unclear, 100,000,000 is very clear. Structure is the way in which you format your response so that it's clear and meaningful to the listener.

Spontaneous structure is simply a way to tell a story. It's a way to explain anything by using simple structure to frame a response. Your challenge, if you want to be engaging, is to find a way to be authentic while using structure to support your ideas. In addition, the confidence you gain by having a structure to your response will come through and build an intellectual and emotional bridge with the listener.

Learn and practice the structures presented here then select one or two that work for you. Get comfortable with those structures and lean on them in situations where you are required to think on your feet and come up with a smart answer quickly.

Here are **five common spontaneous speaking structures** that use the Rule of Three to present a clear, thoughtful, and smart response. When responding, always start by ensuring your questioner that you understand and appreciate their question. Then proceed with your reply.

NOTE: Don't get overwhelmed with so many options. Decide on one or two that would work best for you and practice using them until it feels natural.

(1) Three Whats

What? So What? Now What? I learned this method from Stanford professor Matt Abrahams. This simple framework involves three statements that can easily explain any concept.

What? What happened or what is emerging?

So What? Why is it important or what lessons can we learn from it?

Now What? What are we going to do next as a result, or what should we do to move forward?

EXAMPLE:

Question: The merger is causing a lot of confusion and our customer service people don't have the right answers. How does your plan solve that problem?

Response: Thank you for that question. You make a good point.

WHAT?: As a result of merging the two business units, the product overlap is causing confusion for our own customer service representatives.

SO WHAT?: We quickly realized that with the product launch, we didn't spend enough time training the people who have been on the front line of customer service.

NOW WHAT?: We created a detailed online workshop for our customer service reps, as well as an updated FAQ with the most current information.

(2) P.R.E.P. Approach

P.R.E.P. can be used when someone is questioning your recommendation or reasoning, as it sets up a framework to support your viewpoint. It is also useful in any general feedback session. In this approach, notice you focus on one main point, not three or five.

P – Point: Make your point or answer the question.

R – Reason: Give your reason or explanation regarding the point.

E – Example: Provide an example that supports your position.
P - Point: Conclude by repeating your point.

EXAMPLE:

Question: What do you suggest we do with our ACE product next year?
Response: I'm glad you brought that up.
Point: I suggest we eliminate the ACE product from our catalog completely.
Reason: For the simple reason that the ACE is no longer compatible with the rest of our product line.
Example: For example, our new Hi-Power Battery pack cannot connect to the ACE and is the only product in our line that uses our old battery.
Point: For this reason, we should eliminate it from the catalog.

(3) Timeline

The Timeline structure has a forward dynamic, using time to move ideas through the thought process. Some situations in which it can be used are: Before, During, and After; Last Year, This Year, and Next Year; Start of the Project, Peak of Implementation, and Wrapping Up.

EXAMPLE:

Question: Why does the design of the display box keep changing?
Response: You're right. This is the third change we've had for the box since we launched the product two years ago.
Two years ago, when we started developing this product, Walters, our largest customer, planned to display it on the bottom shelf. We determined the box needed to be at least eighteen inches tall so the buyer would see it as they walked down the aisle.
Last year, Walters decided to increase their order and put the product on the top shelf, but the specifications for that location changed, with the maximum acceptable height at seventeen inches.

And this year, for the holiday season, Walters has given us the great opportunity to display our product on endcaps, which is expected to increase sales by more than 38 percent. To maximize this marketing opportunity, our display box must fit neatly into a fifteen-inch slot.

(4) F.A.T. Method

The F.A.T. Method is a simple way to share your personal feelings or opinions about something. Inherent in the structure is your personal perspective and story that ties back to the question or topic.

F – Feel: Express your honest feelings about the topic.

A – Anecdote: Share a relevant personal story.

T – Tie back: Tie the story back to the topic at hand.

EXAMPLE:

Question: Do you think hiring summer interns helps us be more productive or takes up too much time in training and mentoring?

Response: Thanks for that question.

Feeling. This is something I've grappled with myself. I honestly believe that mentoring young people helps us do a better job because it brings innovative new ideas to our team.

Anecdote. I remember when five interns showed up in my office this past June, and I had to stop everything to introduce them to our team and figure out what they will spend their time doing. I was skeptical, but the following week, all five interns participated in our product innovation meeting. To my surprise, the interns were the ones who came up with the idea of linking our mobile app directly to the network for immediate updates.

Tie back. There is definitely an investment of time with summer interns, but I believe the payback is more than worth it.

(5) Zoom Lens

The Zoom Lens Plan evolves like a camera lens zooming in or out of a discussion. If the level of details required becomes more granular—or the opposite, a bigger picture is needed—this approach is very effective. Some ways it can be applied are: company, department, individual; student, teacher, principal; department budget, regional plan, corporate profits.

EXAMPLE:

Question: How will our organization deal with all the changes this merger will require throughout the company?

Response: Good point. This merger will impact all levels of the organization.

At **the employee level**, we're planning change management workshops that will introduce every employee to the structure of the new organization and answer their questions on the transition.

At **the department level**, managers will be invited to a two-day off-site that will train them on the skills needed to lead and manage the disruption caused by the merger.

And at **the executive level,** we are bringing in a consulting firm to help us integrate the management styles and cultures of the two organizations to ensure a smooth transition.

These are just a few of the many presentation structures that exist. Refer to this Structure Summary chart for a quick breakdown of the ones described above.

Common Speaking Structures Summary

Structure Type	Description	Best Situation for Use
Three Whats	• What?-what happened • So what? -why it's important • Now what?-what the next step is	Explaining an idea and its relevance to the audience
P.R.E.P. Approach	• Your **P**oint • **R**eason for your response • **E**xample leading to point • Repeat your **P**oint	Helping others understand underlying logic
Timeline	Forward-moving timeframe	Good for providing historical perspective
F.A.T. Method	• How you **F**eel about the topic • **A**necdote for additional insight • **T**ie back to original point	Use to influence people to support your idea
ZOOM Lens	Focus IN or OUT of details in a situation	Apply to big story that has consequences at many levels

Structure Sets You Free

By providing meaningful structure in your conversation, you are helping both yourself and your audience. Research shows that people retain structured information up to 40 percent more reliably and accurately than information that is presented in an unstructured manner.

Research shows that people retain structured information up to 40 percent more reliably and accurately than information that is presented in an unstructured manner.

Laying out a presentation or conversation in one of these structures helps you remember what you plan to say, because even if you forget the specifics, you know the general structure. In essence, your structure provides you with a map, making it a little bit harder to get lost.

SUMMARY

To ensure you're providing an excellent answer to the question, you'll need to quickly process what you've learned and what you already know. Using the **Rule of Three** allows you to express concepts simply, emphasizing your points and increasing the memorability of your message. When you apply a structure, you are helping both yourself and your audience remember your key message. And best of all, structure keeps you on track, helps you stay focused, and brings your audience along.

MAKE IT REAL WORKSHEETS

Structure Is the Key to Success

Giving structure to your thoughts helps you stay on track while providing clarity and simplicity for your listener. Even better, when your response is organized, you sound confident and smart. After all, isn't that what you're going for?

The Rule of Three is an important part of a good structure. It allows you to express concepts more completely, emphasize your points, and increase the memorability of your message. It has been proven time and again that three is the most persuasive number in communication. It has a natural rhythm and has been applied in all areas of life for hundreds of years. And that's the truth, the whole truth, and nothing but the truth.

How can you apply the Rule of Three to your work environment?

Focus on your work, your team, your goals.

Apply the Rule of Three to three areas.

EXAMPLE—FOR MY LEADERSHIP WORKSHOPS:

A strong leader motivates, inspires, and coaches their team for success.

Your first Rule of 3: "Motivates" Give an example of how a leader motivates:

____

____

____

____

____

____

____

Your second Rule of 3: "Inspires" Give an example of how a leader inspires:

Your third Rule of 3: "Coaches" Give an example of how a leader coaches:

A Structured Formula

To further develop the **Rule of Three**, we depend on defined structures to help present information in a way that will reinforce its relevance to the topic. For example, the Timeline structure is useful for sharing a story about the evolution of something over time. The F.A.T. Method allows us to easily share personal opinions in a way that ties directly to the original point.

The structures discussed are: (1) Three Whats, (2) P.R.E.P. Approach, (3) Timeline, (4) F.A.T. Method, and (5) Zoom Lens. The key is to find the structures that suit you best—the ones that fit your personal communication style and the situations you typically encounter.

Try out all the structures to feel them in action. Use each in different situations, and the best organization method for you will naturally evolve. Incorporate your favorite structure into your thought process often enough and you will begin to naturally apply it to thinking on your feet in unexpected situations.

Using at least two unique structures, respond to one of these questions:

Why do you feel sales numbers are down?

Why are our customers moving away from our new products and returning to the old?

Why are superhero movies making such a big comeback?

(Feel free to fabricate some facts; the point is to practice the structure.) Refer to pages 82-86.

Using at least two unique structures (different from above), respond to the question:

Has your community taken advantage of people's interest in living a healthier lifestyle? (Feel free to fabricate some facts; the point is to practice the structure.)

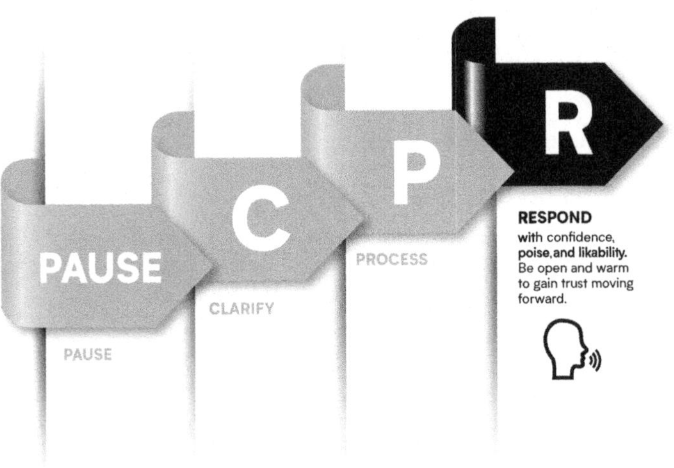
BEFORE YOU SAY ANOTHER WORD
PAUSE & APPLY CPR
PAUSE - CLARIFY - PROCESS - RESPOND
PAUSE
C
P
R
PAUSE
CLARIFY
PROCESS
RESPOND
with confidence, poise, and likability. Be open and warm to gain trust moving forward.

MARCUS GARVEY
Political activist and entrepreneur

Chapter 7

Respond

You paused, listened, and heard the question. You clarified to understand exactly what was being asked. You processed and accessed your own knowledge and expertise. You've organized your thoughts. Now you're ready to respond with confidence, poise, and likeability.

While you may have carefully prepared for your conversation or presentation, it's how you handle yourself when you are least prepared that often demonstrates your leadership and ability to influence others.

It's how you handle yourself when you are least prepared that often demonstrates your leadership.

MAKE AN IMPRESSION

The imprint you leave with people is frequently much more important than the information you give them. Nonverbal gestures, delivery, eye contact, and body language all make an impression.

Be likeable. This isn't a popularity contest, but being likeable is winning half the battle of influencing others. What counts in the end is not so much what you say as how you say it. The

This isn't a popularity contest, but being likeable is winning half the battle.

tremendous amount of information that you communicate about yourself nonverbally is reflected in your delivery. Many people give mediocre responses with superb delivery, and they generally fare better than those with strong responses and mediocre delivery skills.

People like people who like them. Let them know you genuinely like them. Maintaining eye contact shows respect for your audience. It shows sincerity, truth, and conviction in what you are saying. Remember to smile, welcoming the question and the interaction.

Maximize Your Nonverbals

If you keep your cool, you will keep your power. People can't read your mind, so you must convey that you're relaxed not only with your words but also with your face and body language.

Your face tells a story. One of the most effective ways to demonstrate confidence and poise is literally right under your nose . . . it's your face. Even without uttering a word, people will form an opinion of you just by looking at your face. But under the stress of thinking on your feet, we tend to forget that the face is sending messages that may be even more powerful than the words we choose to use in that stressful moment. Basically, there are three possible facial positions or expressions: the closed face, the bland face, and the open face.

The closed face results from the creation of a vertical line between the brows. It's the frown line. Many people do this when they think. It's not effective or likeable to do in front of others or when thinking on your feet because it often conveys worry, confusion, or anger.

The bland face has a monotone look. Some call it the frozen face because there is limited to no muscle movement. It is an expressionless face—nothing moves but the mouth. Unfortunately, due to nervousness, many exhibit this lack of expression when speaking in a public setting.

The open face has slightly elevated eyebrows, creating horizontal lines on the forehead. It naturally appears in animated conversations or when telling a favorite story. People who speak with an open face appear to be honest, believable, trustworthy, confident, and self-assured. It has the power to shift a negative conversation into a positive mode.

Your body talks. When under pressure in the workplace and stressful thoughts dominate your mind, your body gets rigid and you stop using gestures. However, if you want to appear comfortable and natural, you need to relax and consciously force yourself to gesture. Your gestures are perceived by others as a burst of energy. It's the communicator's equivalent of a hug. People who gesture appear more relaxed and comfortable.

Just like you want to have an open face, the key to strong body language is to stay open. Therefore, you want to avoid crossing your arms, hunching your shoulders, and turning your body away from your audience. If you're sitting or standing in an open position, you're signaling strength. Sit up straight with your chest out and shoulders back. If you're standing, plant your feet shoulder-width apart. Imagine a cape flowing behind you with your hands on your hips. It's as if you are proclaiming, *"Go ahead and shoot your arrows. They can't hurt me. But if they do, I'm strong enough to take it."* Incidentally, there is something magical about open posture, for when you look strong, you feel strong. And pretty soon that strength will become real.

Your voice can win the day. When your face is open and your body is open, your voice takes on the warmest tone. Your volume, pitch, and rate are important characteristics of an effective response. Speak loud enough for your audience to hear you and soft enough to draw them into you. Your pitch and rate should be comfortable to your audience. Any extremes will cause your audience to focus on how you are delivering your response instead of the response itself.

GET A GRIP

Nervous? Of course, you're nervous. Most people are when they're on the spot or caught off guard.

Most people get anxious in those brief moments before they're about to present or discuss something of importance. Knowing your turn is next or seeing a raised hand in the audience might trigger a nervous reaction like gurgling of your stomach, racing of your heart, legs feeling wobbly and beginning to shake, or perspiration spreading. Then your mind gets in on the action. You think, *Oh my goodness, this is not going to go well.* And things continue to spiral out of control.

YOUR ANXIETY SHOWS, AND IT'S NOT PRETTY

When you're nervous, you're likely to repeat words, fidget, lose eye contact, sway, pace, and talk too fast . . . You get the idea. What should you do?

Fake it till you make it. You may not be feeling confident, but it's best to keep that to yourself. Here are some suggestions to convey a confident presence whether you're feeling it or not.

You may not be feeling confident, but it's best to keep that to yourself.

Look 'Em in the Eye

Confident speakers connect with their audience through consistent eye contact. Scientific evidence suggests eye contact makes a person appear more approachable. In the West, we have sayings like: "Look me in the eyes so I know you're telling the truth," or "Eyes are the windows to the soul." We also know that the lack of good eye contact—or worse yet, rapidly darting glances—makes you appear nervous, deceptive, or both. And finally, not looking at your audience causes them to feel excluded, which invites feelings of subliminal resentment toward you.

Be sure to lock in and maintain eye contact. If you feel uncomfortable looking people in the eye, then you must figure out a way to fake it. When looking at people on an individual basis, try looking at the spot between their eyebrows. If you are speaking to a group, scan just above their heads. Amazingly, it looks as if you're looking right into their eyes. Be sure to spread your eye contact around so you connect with everyone.

Stand Tall

Confident speakers avoid distracting body movements. Swaying or leaning is actually self-soothing, much like when a baby sucks their thumb. However, these behaviors signal discomfort and nervousness to the audience. To eliminate unneeded and distracting movement, face your feet forward directly under your shoulders, bend your knees slightly, and move one foot an inch ahead of the other. From this position, it is very hard to sway or lean.

In addition, nervous speakers sometimes retreat and unintentionally take a step back when challenged. This sends a negative message to the audience. Instead, you need to stand upright and take one step toward your audience when you begin speaking. Leaning in and approaching your audience makes you appear confident and embracing.

Standing tall allows you to breathe fully and maximize your voice. In fact, research suggests that people who maximize the full extent of their bodies and the space around them are seen as more powerful and persuasive. Interestingly, the very act of taking up more space makes you feel more powerful. Consider making a wide gesture. You might say, "Most people here . . ." as you spread your arms and make eye contact throughout the room.

Leaning in and approaching your audience makes you appear confident and embracing.

Words Matter

Sometimes your lack of confidence creeps in simply by the words you choose. Rather than declare something authoritatively, you use phrases that soften your position, such as *"I think," "sort of,"* or *"you know"* to respond to comments or questions. In a casual discussion, these might help by allowing you to appear less dogmatic and open to collaboration. However, in public presentations or when responding to critical comments, these phrases reduce your authority and can make you sound wishy-washy.

The best way to address this is with word substitution. Find the words to replace less assertive ones with confident phrases. For example, *"I think"* becomes *"I believe"* or *"I know."* The phrases *"kind of"* or *"sort of"* can be replaced with *"one way"* (e.g., *"This approach should sort of help"* becomes, *"One way to help is . . ."*). Finding more assertive substitutions affords you a way to make your point more clearly and definitively.

It Works

Since your audience does not know you are faking behavior that makes you appear competent and confident, they treat you as if you are naturally assured, which in turn fuels your feelings of competence and confidence. Try it. "Fake it till you make it" really works!

MAKE YOUR AUDIENCE COMFORTABLE

Think about it: What does it feel like when you're sitting in the audience and watching a nervous or anxious speaker? For most people, it's difficult. It feels uncomfortable and awkward. Since most audiences are made up of kind, empathetic people who want the speaker to succeed, they try to help a nervous speaker gain composure and calm down, often by averting their gaze, distracting themselves by looking at their phones, or casually chatting with each other. Unfortunately, a nervous speaker witnessing these audience behaviors views the audience as disengaged and uninvolved, which only makes the speaker more nervous.

The best way to avoid this awkward, anxiety-induced audience disconnection is to realize that your primary job as a speaker is to make your audience comfortable. If they are comfortable, they can pay attention and connect to you and your content.

> ***Your primary job as a speaker is to make your audience comfortable.***

In order to make your audience comfortable, you must reject the mistaken assumption that most speakers make. Speakers tend to assume that giving a presentation is about them as speakers; demonstrating their depth of knowledge, articulating thoughts, and witty commentary. This rarely works. A better approach is to focus on the audience. The best speakers never ask themselves, *What do I want to say?* Instead they ask, *What does my audience need to hear or learn?*

Connect with your audience. By focusing on your audience's needs, you remove yourself from the spotlight. Their needs are paramount. In taking this audience-focused approach, you not only engage your audience more since you're giving them what they need, but you will present content that supports their perspective so they can truly appreciate and understand your message. This approach makes your audience more comfortable and open to receiving your message more readily.

Asking your audience a question and giving them something to think about or respond to is a great way to convert from presentation mode to conversation mode. This turns a "me vs. you moment" into an "us discussion." Having some relevant statistics at hand will also help you confidently move the conversation in the direction you desire while appearing knowledgeable and relatable.

Asking your audience a question turns a "me vs. you moment" into an "us discussion."

Here is an example when speaking to an audience about productivity:

"How many of you have a calendar filled with back-to-back meetings?" (Typically, all hands are raised.)

"How many of you feel you have more than enough time each day to focus on your own priorities?" (Typically, most hands come down.)

"You're not alone. Seventy-eight percent of professionals say there aren't enough hours in the day to devote to their most important tasks. Well, that's what I'm here to help you with today."

OK! NOW YOU'RE READY TO START THE CONVERSATION

As suggested by Dr. Matt Abrahams, simply begin your reply to the question or comment as if it were a natural conversation with a friend or colleague.

In order to be more conversational, use informal language that helps you connect with your audience and feels more inclusive. A nervous or inexperienced speaker often tries to sound smart and uses words that alienate or disengage the audience. Rather than saying, *"The ramifications of that elucidation were pure pandemonium,"* you might say, *"That solution resulted in chaos."* Being conversational not only connects you with the audience and helps them understand your point but the natural interaction will also help you manage any anxiety.

While statistics or surprising facts are a good way to start the conversation, a thought-provoking concept is another way to get your audience personally engaged. In a recent leadership meeting about the need to focus and move our success forward, the speaker asked the group to reflect on this statement: *"If you don't work toward achieving your own goals, you are destined to work toward achieving the goals of others."* He then solicited several people to share their interpretation of the concept. This turned a presentation-response into a conversation-response. Everyone was seeking to find, share, and be part of the solution.

Pause: The Loudest Nonverbal Cue

There's more to your message than words. Your message is not conveyed only by your words but also by your pauses. A pause isn't a moment of nothing. Used strategically, it is a tool to help you build intellectual and emotional connection with your audience.

When you pause, you give your audience time to process what you have just said. A pause allows your listeners to stay engaged and enables them to follow what comes next. If you still don't get it, reread *Chapter 4: Pause!*

The Right Structure

Remember that structure is the key to success. Whether you apply the basic Rule of Three or use a specific structure that suits your situation, add a pause between ideas so your audience can easily follow. Without the pause, the listener may miss your transition and be unable to identify each idea. Refer to *Chapter 6: Process* for structure ideas that will add credibility and power to your response.

Consider repeating the specific words or ideas used by the questioner in your response to let them know you were really listening. Also be sure to maintain good eye contact, a comfortable stance, and a friendly, open face. Use these fundamentals to keep your response on track, relevant, positive, and succinct.

> ***Repeat the specific words or ideas used by the questioner in your response to let them know you were really listening.***

Use the Muscle of Others

On occasion, you may not be the best one to answer the question. Perhaps a member of the audience is an expert and you believe he is willing and eager to respond. Consider redirecting the question but do so only if you follow Marian Woodall's rules below.

The Rules of Redirecting

The rules of redirecting the question to another person, either one of your colleagues or someone in the audience, embody the Golden

Rule for responders, "Do unto others as you would have them do unto you." There are four aspects:

1. Get the attention of the person to whom you are redirecting. Begin by saying their name loudly and clearly so they are alert to what is about to happen.
2. Repeat the question clearly. They may not have heard it.
3. Buy them some time. Give an explanation about their expert background. You're also justifying why you aren't answering the question.
4. Identify the questioner, if possible.

Redirecting the question can strengthen a team. It can also be a gesture of goodwill or be considered a compliment. Examine your audience, determine your options, and share the spotlight when you can.

And as always, delivery counts. Redirect the question with a confident tone and a strong presence. Otherwise you may appear unprepared.

When You're Done, Stop

Too often, Marian Woodall writes, people give a quality response with the right amount of information and the appropriate tone then blow it all by babbling on beyond the finish or by shrugging at the end.

But I'm not sure if that's what you want to know . . .

However, I haven't really studied that aspect yet . . .

I really don't have a strong opinion on that . . .

If you can't figure out a way to stop, try this trick: repeat the essence of the question as a close. *"So that's why we decided to abandon the project."*

UNLEASH THE POWER OF STORIES

A compelling story can turn an ordinary presentation into an exceptional one. Why? Because stories engage an audience, evoke empathy, increase trust, and motivate action.

Virtually from the time we learn to communicate, we're listening to and telling stories. Even as adults, stories stick in our minds, leaving impressions long after we first hear them.

According to a Harvard study co-authored by renowned professor Amy Cuddy, leaders need to project warmth to connect to their audience; projecting competence alone is not sufficient for most leaders to succeed. Although projecting competence is clearly important, neglecting to demonstrate trustworthiness, warmth, and experience makes it very difficult to gain loyalty and be persuasive in a meaningful way. This is where a good story can really help.

Business, after all, isn't just about numbers and data. It's about people, situations, conflict, empathy, drama, comedy, and countless other human interactions. Storytelling is too often overlooked as a business technique.

Whether you know it or not, most people are natural storytellers, and when they tell stories, they smile, show emotion, and radiate authenticity. Not only is authenticity engaging and persuasive but the storyteller feels infinitely more comfortable and confident when they're just being themselves.

Telling a story doesn't take a lot of memorization; you already know it. And your audience is much more likely to remember key facts if they are tied to a story. In fact, research shows that people are twenty-two times more likely to remember figures, statistics, and data when they're incorporated into a narrative.

People are twenty-two times more likely to remember figures, statistics, and data when they're incorporated into a narrative.

When we tell stories, we're conversational. We naturally smile, use good body language, and make eye contact—all the things that build trust with the audience. As your audience engages back with interest and positive feedback, your confidence rises and your points can be made effortlessly while being easily understood.

And finally, you have plenty to choose from: a lifetime of personal and professional stories about events that have happened to you or to those you know.

Fortunately, if you are not a born storyteller, the ability to tell a story successfully can be learned. Maximize your effectiveness by learning how to tell powerful and persuasive stories.

Choose Your Story Wisely

The best stories come from your own experience—from things with which you already have an emotional connection. When you recount something that's happened to you, you'll recall not just the events but also the feelings associated with them. That will color your stories with natural expression, feeling, and movement.

The most effective stories are usually the most ordinary ones because you want your narrative to resonate with your audience on an emotional level. Few people can relate to the time you rode a camel in Petra, but everyone can relate to the time you were stranded in a storm, getting soaking wet.

Few people can relate to the time you rode a camel in Petra, but everyone can relate to the time you were stranded in a storm.

Choose a story that illustrates the point you're trying to make. Although stories can be entertaining, that is not the point. Be sure your story brings the listener back to your message.

Tell It Like It Is

Storytelling has been used since the beginning of time in every culture and passed down through family generations. Now it's gaining popularity with business and commercial presentations. Tech giant Cisco Systems used to deliver fact-heavy presentations promoting their products. Then they noticed that when they stopped listing features and started telling stories, they became much more effective and successful. For instance, by telling the story of a struggling local small business owner who grew his company and managed it more effectively using Cisco products, the company was able to humanize information about technology and make their benefits more relatable.

Although it's true every story has three key aspects—a beginning, a middle, and an end—I propose that, in fact, there are four parts to every good story:

1. Set the scene.
2. Build toward the conflict.
3. Hit the climax.
4. Connect the dots.

Here is a true story about my personal experience last winter.

Part 1: Set the scene. The first thing to do as you begin to tell your story is set up the narrative. Give your listener the context, situation, environment, time frame—any information they'll need in order to understand the story. You might also start with your main point.

Things aren't always as they appear. I was skiing at Vail, a fancy upscale ski resort with lots of wealthy and demanding people wearing expensive clothes and living the good life. I was there to speak at a conference for one day. After my presentation, I was waiting for the busy airport shuttle.

Part 2: Build toward the conflict. Once you've set the scene, begin to tell the audience what happened. Be sure to use play-by-play action, language, and dialogue.

When the shuttle arrived, it was nearly full and barely had one seat left for me. The one available seat was on the bench behind the driver. Two people were already seated on the three-person bench. The attractive woman was wearing a stunning fur coat and the man, seated closest to the door, was dressed in a name-brand sweater, both just reeking of wealth. Neither looked at me as I tried to find my seat. Finally, I said: "Do you mind if I squeeze in next to you?" The man did not say a word nor did he move a muscle as I squeezed into barely half a seat next to him on the bench.

I was furious, thinking: Who do they think they are? Entitled to the entire space with no consideration for others. Must be a good life skiing at Vail, enjoying all the benefits of the one percent. I was fuming.

Part 3: Hit the climax. This is the peak of the conflict. You should be clear and concise with just a few lines of action or dialogue.

Not only was I squeezed into the seat but the bicycle tires propped next to the driver's seat were pressing against my legs. I was enraged. Such privilege, *I thought.*

Suddenly, the man, who hadn't moved a muscle, turned to me and said, "Oh, excuse me. Are my wheelchair tires pushing against your legs? I'm so sorry."

Part 4: Connect the dots. Interpret the meaning of the story and connect it to the issue you're discussing.

What? He's in a wheelchair? He's paraplegic? The reason he didn't move a muscle is because he couldn't move a muscle! Boy, was I off base!

We so often jump to conclusions based on our own biases and limited perspective. In order to be successful as an innovative team, we must set our biases aside and evaluate the whole picture using all the facts, not just our assumptions.

Secret Ingredients

Help them visualize.

Use visualization to dramatize boring facts and figures. Help the listener visualize the story and be in the moment with you.

Instead of: *He was really angry.*

How about: *He stormed out, slammed the door, and kicked the mailbox.*

Instead of: *We're expecting to sell an additional five hundred thousand units after the launch of the new ad campaign.*

How about: *Imagine the large conference center in this building filled with our new BreatheOn product wall to wall, floor to ceiling. That's how many additional units we will put in the hands of people suffering from lung disease next year.*

Speak from within the Experience.

Instead of: *I had to get out of there as fast as I could.*

How about: *I jumped in my truck, heart pounding, palms sweating as I fumbled for my keys and sped away.*

Shock the Audience. Build Up to an Unexpected Event.

He was paraplegic. He didn't move a muscle because he couldn't move a muscle.

The End: Begin with the end in mind. Share your purpose up front. My story started with: Things aren't always what they seem. I'd like to share a story about my trip to Vail Ski Resort last winter.

The Moral

All stories need a purpose, moral, or lesson, and your listeners will count on you to provide the point of view and spell out the moral message. The clarity and strength you bring to the telling will give the listeners a sense of comfort and understanding.

If you're not telling a story with an unexpected twist, consider preparing for questions and comments by collecting a few surprising statistics you can use in response. Here are some startling business facts:

- A *Harvard Business Review* survey reveals **58 percent of people say they trust strangers more than their own boss**. This is truly shocking. We live in a world where cultural trust is at an all-time low. And distrust of leadership should be worrisome to all of us who are working to motivate our teams to success.
- According to Marketing Donut, **92 percent of salespeople quit after they are told NO four times by a prospect; however, 80 percent of prospects say no at least four times before they say yes.** What does this mean for you? It means you must get very comfortable with hearing the word "no" and with the feeling of rejection. Think of it this way: the more nos you hear, the closer you are to a yes.
- **Almost 90 percent of workers are not actively engaged in their jobs**, according to Gallup. Not only does a lack of employee engagement result in decreased productivity, it also causes high turnover.

Get to the Point

Here's a story I might use in response to a question or comment about needing to trust our gut or taking a risk with creativity.

I recently had the opportunity to visit an elementary school in my community interested in doing a workshop on creativity. I visited the kindergarten class and watched as all the children were busy drawing pictures with colorful markers and glittery stickers. As we passed by the desk of one adorable little girl, the teacher asked, *"Penelope, what are you drawing a picture of?"*

"I'm drawing a picture of God," Penelope replied.

"Really?" responded the teacher. *"But nobody knows what God looks like."*

"Well," confidently replied Penelope, *"they will in a minute!"*

If only we could be as secure and self-assured as we all were as children, we'd have the confidence to share creative ideas and find simple solutions for our biggest challenges.

The message: Let's bring out the creative juices we've suppressed and be open to hearing each other's ideas no matter how crazy or counterintuitive they seem.

Use Analogies

When it comes to creating effective understanding, analogies are hard to beat. Most of their persuasive power comes from the audience arriving at the intended understanding on their own, says Brian Clark, author of *CopyBlogger.*

In response to someone making a claim that seems difficult to believe or extremely unlikely, I'd like to share Brian Clark's story:

An elderly man storms into his doctor's office, steaming mad. "Doc, my new twenty-two-year-old wife is expecting a baby. You performed my vasectomy thirty years ago, and I'm very upset right now."

"Let me respond to that by telling you a story," the doctor calmly replies.

"A hunter once accidentally left the house with an umbrella instead of his rifle. Out of nowhere, a bear surprised him in the woods . . . so the hunter pointed the umbrella, fired, and killed the bear."

"Impossible," the old man snaps back. "Someone else must have shot the bear."

"And there you have it," the doctor says.

Of course, there are plenty of analogies that are much simpler than an entire story. For example, I recently heard a presentation on health insurance that began with: "Living without health insurance is like pitching a tent at the edge of a mountain and hoping it doesn't get too windy."

When asked, *"How did this updated insurance program gain so much popularity?"* the speaker replied, *"The basic recipe stayed the same, but the new filing features were like adding chocolate chips to the plain vanilla batter. It made the new process a lot easier to swallow."*

Entertaining stories and descriptive analogies are the bedrock of memorable communication. Share a new concept, wrap it in a comfortable, warm blanket of understanding, and the listener will happily follow you to your conclusion.

Entertaining stories and descriptive analogies are the bedrock of memorable communication.

SUMMARY

Your goal is to respond with confidence and poise! Start by taming your inner nervousness and focus on making the audience comfortable. There is some truth to the saying *"Fake it till you make it."* Research shows that acting courageous in the face of fear actually reduces the anxiety you feel and helps you become bolder. Fight your own negative self-talk with positive affirmations. Look your audience in the eye and stand tall as you express your thoughts with confidence.

Make it a conversation. Engage your audience. Ask a question or pose a thought-provoking comment. Be likeable. Have an open face, lean in, and smile. Let them know you are interested in them, you're happy to be there, and you want to solve their problem.

If you have a good one, tell your story. Stories leave a lasting impression and show people how numbers, data, facts, and figures impact real people and daily life. Be sure your story has a point and share it up front. Set the scene, build toward the conflict, hit the climax, and finally, connect the dots. Bring the audience along for the ride and you will likely win them over.

When you're done responding, stop! Let your confidence show as your words sink in.

MAKE IT REAL WORKSHEETS

Respond with Confidence and Poise

At this point, you understand the fundamentals of thinking on your feet: pause, listen, question, process, and use a powerful structure to organize your thoughts. Now the moment has arrived. It's time to respond with confidence and poise.

Set yourself up for success by connecting with your audience as soon as you begin. The best part of all is that when you connect with your audience, you begin to relax. You exude confidence and are well on your way to success.

Think about a common situation where you find yourself in a thinking-on-your-feet moment. It could be at work, a community event, a family gathering, a personal conversation, or other. How can you use each one of these techniques?

Ask a thought-provoking question.

Take a poll that gets everyone involved.

Set up the topic with an analogy.

Share a relevant or surprising statistic.

Analogies are a powerful and influential tool. An opinionated statement on its own does not make nearly the same impact as an analogy, such as Forrest Gump's famous line *"Life is like a box of chocolates. You never know what you're going to get."*

What are several examples of analogies that are relevant to your world? Come up with one or two powerful ideas, and you will likely use them many times over in your conversations and responses.

____

____

Your Story: The Most Memorable Part of Your Presentation

A compelling story will turn an ordinary presentation into an exceptional one. Stories engage the audience, evoke empathy, and add an element of entertainment to a presentation of facts and data.

Your stories make you likeable. Your stories make you fun. Your stories make people want to listen to what you have to say. Your stories are sometimes more important than your facts. Your stories drive the point home.

Personal stories are the best, although I've used stories I've read in articles, found online, or have had shared with me over time. Anywhere you can find a good story, take note and be sure to give credit where it's due.

Review these prompts to identify hidden stories you might want to develop and share with others. Any story with an element of surprise has the potential to teach a lesson and leave a lasting impression.

Come up with your own stories. Think about:

What motivates you? How does it motivate you?

What role does procrastination play in your life? How have you experienced it?

When have you been a leader?

When did you have to perform under pressure?

What risks have you taken?

What failures have led to the most growth?

When have you been brave?
What challenges have you overcome?
When did you find that things were not as they appeared to be?
When was the last time you left your comfort zone?
What are you most proud of?
What are you least proud of?
When did you succeed when you thought you might fail?
When did you do something nice for a stranger?
When did a stranger do something nice for you?
Who are your heroes?
What crazy social media situation have you found yourself in?
What movies have made an impact on you?
What are your favorite books? Are there stories worth repeating?
What is a memorable high school moment?
What are your hidden talents? Have you shown them?
Where have you traveled? What experiences have you had?

Develop Your Story

Stories have been a part of human development and culture for thousands of years. Stories are the basis of laws, rules of engagement, moral lessons, and pure entertainment. Tell a good story and your message will have a stronger appeal.

The story should move easily and quickly through four stages:

- Set the scene. Explain the situation, context, and people involved.
- Build toward action/conflict. Explain what happened and move toward discomfort, action, or conflict of the situation.
- Hit the climax/surprise. What's the big moment? The unexpected surprise?
- Connect the dots. Explain the moral or lesson learned. Bring it full circle as to how it relates to the conversation at hand.

Use this template to develop your story.

List main ideas and details that help the listener imagine the scene, clarify the situation, and bring them along on the journey to the climax. Set the scene:

____

____

____

Build toward the conflict: What happened? How does the story flow?

____

____

____

What's the climax, the surprise?

____

____

____

What's the lesson learned, the moral of the story?

____

____

____

PART 3
Now You're Killin' It

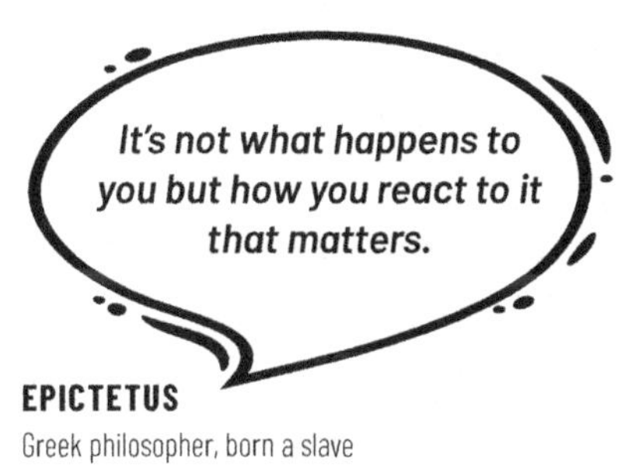

EPICTETUS
Greek philosopher, born a slave

Chapter 8

The Best and the Worst That Can Happen

THAT'S SO NICE OF YOU TO SAY!

What if the person you are listening to is giving you a compliment?

We all like to be noticed and acknowledged for our accomplishments. So, you would think accepting a compliment would be pretty simple. Someone says something nice. You say: *"Thank you."* End of story.

But unfortunately, the story often unfolds like it did for my colleague Jessica. After presenting her final project results to the team, our colleague commented: *"Wow, that's amazing. I can see how much effort you put into it and the great results you got are impressive. I'll have to take some lessons from you."*

Jessica's response: *"Oh, it wasn't that much work. I was hoping for better results and you could definitely do this too."*

WHY DID YOU JUST SAY THAT? This makes me want to scream!

Accepting Compliments Is Good for Your Career

By negating the compliment, Jessica dismisses her own abilities and worth—and also her teammates' opinion. By suggesting that the project was so easy and anyone could do it (which, of course, was not true), Jessica implied that anyone could do her job. *"Oh, no big deal."* Is this the image she wants to paint of herself? This is no way to get appreciated, much less recognized for a job well done.

When you devalue a compliment, you send the message that you have low self-esteem, you aren't confident in your work, or worse, you don't respect the opinion of the person who gave you the praise. On the other hand, graciously accepting a compliment is good for your self-confidence and can boost your career and improve your working relationships.

Graciously accepting a compliment is good for your self-confidence and can boost your career and improve your working relationships.

"Thank You" Is a Full Sentence

The proper response to any compliment is *"thank you."* It's a simple and powerful phrase. You can further express your gratitude by saying, *"Thank you. That's very kind of you,"* or *"Thank you. I appreciate the compliment."*

If you feel you need to say more, you can add a neutral statement that supports the compliment without arrogance or conceit. You might say: *"Thank you. I really enjoyed working on this project,"* or *"It was challenging, but it all came together in the end."*

Be sure your body language doesn't give the wrong impression. Don't cross your arms or appear disinterested due to your own discomfort. Instead, maintain eye contact, lean slightly forward, and engage those around you with a warm facial expression. Enjoy the moment of your praise. You deserve it.

Remember to share the spotlight. It's never appropriate to hog all the credit, as it's rarely an individual effort. If you led a team effort, by all means accept the accolade and don't downplay your role. But be sure to also acknowledge the contributions of others. "Joy, Jared, Mark, and I enjoyed putting this program together."

The truth is, when someone notices and appreciates something you've done, they're usually being honest. So, when you receive a compliment, believe it, share it, and take it for what it is—a verbal pat on the back. You're receiving an accolade that's well-deserved.

UH-OH! I DON'T KNOW THAT

You thought you prepared for every possible question, yet there's still that one detail that slipped by. *"Where did that question come from?" "How did I miss that?"*

Most of the time it's no big deal when you don't have a solid answer right away. But sometimes a question can really stump you, and defaulting to *"I don't know"* or *"I'll get back to you"* can risk diminishing your credibility, especially if those are your go-to responses every time you're put on the spot.

Here are some suggestions.

Answer from Your Own Level

No matter what level you are within an organization, whether you're a senior executive, manager, or individual contributor, you typically have a broad understanding of your team's work, but the details in your head are those that revolve around the work you do daily. An executive may focus on the big picture and be less informed about the specific technical details of the product or project he is responsible for. A project analyst keenly understands the data but may be less informed about the future strategy of a product.

I recently worked with Eric, a marketing executive who came across a question about a specific target market. Although this target market was in his area of responsibility, his position required him to work on the big picture, the overall strategy for the region as a whole. In his wisdom, he acknowledged the specific question but then elevated the answer to something he was familiar with. He responded *"I understand your concern about that target market. But I think the bigger issue you've raised is..."* By recognizing and referring to the specific question, he showed respect for the questioner and then elevated the question to the issue as he saw it, demonstrating leadership, knowledge, and confidence.

Not Your Area of Expertise?

If a question is outside your field of expertise, showcase your collaboration and teamwork skills by asking a team or audience member with the relevant credentials to answer it.

For example, if you're an engineer and someone asks a financial question, you can redirect the question to someone you know is from the finance area. You might say something like: *"Carolyn, you're a CPA. Do you have a rough idea how we would calculate the profitability of this project?"* Or, *"Are there any financial people in the audience who might want to guesstimate those numbers?"*

Don't Get Stuck in the Past

If you're asked your opinion about a subject you haven't thought much about, struggling to think of a time you've experienced or come across the situation may be a challenge in the moment. Instead, listen in the moment and then immediately look to the future.

Let's say you're talking about managing change in your dynamic business environment, when someone asks you: *"Do you think business leaders should expect their teams to get on board with new corporate procedures without question or discussion?"* If you try to recall a previous example to reflect on, you may find yourself in a maze of confusion and come up with a weak example. Instead, you might answer more hypothetically and strike a positive, forward-looking note at the same time. So, for example, you might acknowledge how leaders could be tempted to move forward when a corporate mandate has been given but then develop a hypothetical scenario for a more interactive approach to managing change within the team. The point is not to come up with the one right answer but an answer that will respond to the needs of the audience at that time.

The point is not to come up with the one right answer but an answer that will respond to the needs of the audience at that time.

Don't Speculate about Others

Occasionally, you'll get asked a question about your competitors or other experts in the field. Don't respond on anyone else's behalf; instead, use this as an opportunity to share your thoughts about the direction of the industry, topic, products, or leadership.

For example, if you're asked: *"I see your competitor lowered their prices last week. Why do you think they did that?"* You might respond, *"I can't speak to their reasoning or rationale, but when we look at pricing, we take into consideration these factors . . ."*

Be Confident and Candid

It's impossible to prepare for every potential question. Nobody's perfect, and every once in a while, you're going to be asked a perfectly legitimate question that you just can't answer. In this situation, just admit it in a matter-of-fact way without feigning embarrassment, disappointment, or any other negative reaction.

When this happens, first acknowledge the value of the question. *"That's a fair question, and it deserves a fair answer—one that I don't have right now. Let me take a minute to jot a note and I promise to get back to you by this day/week. Will that work?"* Your commitment to explore it further based on the validity of the inquiry demonstrates respect for the questioner and your determination to find the best solution possible.

Keep in mind, your managers, peers, and clients don't expect you to have an encyclopedic mind or never make a mistake. More than anything, they give you their trust when they see how you evaluate and tackle problems as they arise.

WHAT IF YOU BLANK OUT?

No matter how much you prepare, what techniques you use or advice you get, nothing guarantees that you won't forget something you intended to say. So, what should you do if and when you blank out? Most important, remind yourself that your audience knows only what you tell them, not what you intended to tell them. If you forget something, the only person who knows is you.

On the other hand, if you lose your concentration and get off track—and find yourself struggling to get back on track—focus on what you've just said. Instead of trying to figure out what you need to say next: reorient yourself by looking to what you said previously.

In this situation, you might simply paraphrase your previous comments or review your overall speaking idea: *"So you can see that (insert idea) is at the core of what we are talking about."*

THAT QUESTION IS INAPPROPRIATE!

Inappropriate questions are those you may be able to answer, but you choose not to for any number of reasons. The question might reference confidential information, undisclosed facts, private estimates, sensitive pricing, or people issues. You may be tempted to say: *"That's none of your business."* But resist that temptation. Instead, politely respond: *"This information is classified."* Or *"Those figures haven't been released yet."*

Your tone of voice is important. You don't want to embarrass anyone or give the impression that you are above answering the query. Be sure to give the seeker the chance to save face. Let them know you understand their interest, however . . .

DON'T LET NEGATIVITY DERAIL YOU

Occasionally, an audience member's negative comments can set a sour tone or derail a presentation. There could be many reasons for the negative attitude that have nothing to do with you or your presentation—dissatisfaction with the company, frustration with their own personal life or career, a previous unrelated conversation that didn't go well, etc. You have no control over these factors. The only thing you can control is your reaction and behavior in response to the moment. They might say:

"That's ridiculous! We can't possibly have the new product ready in time for the annual convention! Is anyone else stupid enough to think we'll be ready?"

Or . . .

"I can see your arguments for suggesting this protocol. But I think the previous plan was better and you're not going to convince me otherwise!"

Tension and conflict in important meetings are not completely unexpected. In fact, conflict can sometimes be the quickest and best way to make significant progress. You certainly don't want everyone to say yes or blindly agree to all proposals without proper discussion. However, if personality differences or simply a bad attitude is at the root of disruptive comments, turning around these potentially disastrous situations is critical to your presentation and personal success.

Everything comes back to you. Your behavior and reaction are important, especially in this day of digital documentation. Your reaction and response are more crucial than ever. What you think is a closed-door conversation can easily be creatively summarized and posted on social media. You do not want to burn bridges with someone who may have social or professional influence over you in the future.

Your behavior and reaction are important, especially in this day of digital documentation.

In a moment of ugly confrontation, everything feels heightened. You have adrenaline surging through your body, your heart is pumping double-time, and your insides are quivering with rage. Take a moment to breathe (and breathe again) and consider the moment. Your behavior right now will set the tone in the room and reflect on your own character and, in some cases, your leadership abilities.

Avoid repeating either their negative words or their negative tone. Your goal is to respond so that the focus on the question itself becomes positive. Breathe again and try one of these techniques:

Restate and Reframe

How many times have you wondered, *How did we get here? This discussion has nothing to do with our original direction.* If things have gone way off track, you might simply restate the issue being discussed. This helps people refocus, defuse an emotional moment, or take the pressure off responding to a comment that's not relevant to the topic.

If the comment is relevant but simply negative in its approach, best start by rephrasing or repeating the question in a less negative way. For example, in the previous example, regarding having the new product ready, you might begin your response with: *"Sounds like you are concerned that our fast-growing manufacturing team will have trouble meeting this aggressive deadline."*

Ask Probing Questions

Use of well thought-out, probing questions can help divulge what someone is really thinking. Use questions for enlightenment or clarification, not as battering rams. For example, in the above statement about protocol, you might ask: *"Interesting. What do you feel are the important features of the previous plan that won't be a part of the new protocol?"*

Or you might ask for clarification of the comment or word that seems disrespectful or negative. *"Which actions do you find to be ridiculous?"* A further explanation often provides clearer details that are less inflammatory when revisiting the comment.

Facilitate a Positive Conversation

Find the wording or perspective that helps clarify and somewhat neutralize the disparity of ideas. *"What I think you're saying is . . ."* Or, *"What I see happening is . . ."* Or, *"It seems to me that these two positions . . ."* The most successful leaders have a genuine interest in the group's goals and achieving positive outcomes. Facilitating a positive discussion demonstrates an authentic interest in the participants and often diffuses anger and negativity.

Facilitating a positive discussion demonstrates an authentic interest in the participants and often diffuses anger and negativity.

Reorganize and Depersonalize

Direct the conversation away from personal concerns by focusing on process. For example, you might say, *"We seem to agree on the what but are having difficulty with the how."* In this way, you cut the problem in half and narrow the focus of the response.

Depersonalization involves wording the issues so it moves away from personal opinion. For example, as in the previous comment regarding protocol, you might respond: *"So what you're saying is that while the new protocol has strengths, the previous protocol had certain features that are more important."* From here, you can move the conversation into an objective discussion of the relative importance of the different features.

Remember to stay away from "you" accusations. Instead of saying: *"You made a mistake,"* you might state: *"A mistake was made."*

Appeal to Higher Goals

Even when you disagree with what someone is saying, or if you dislike their approach, you can still support the person's right to an opinion and the importance of being heard. Acknowledge their comments without endorsing what they are saying. Agree with them as far as you can then rephrase using less loaded language.

Petty differences, minor power plays, hidden agendas, and personality issues can fade when participants rediscover the real reason for the meeting or presentation. It is a wise and powerful leader who can refocus a meeting by thoughtfully emphasizing the group's higher goals and everyone's areas of agreement.

It is a wise and powerful leader who can refocus a meeting by thoughtfully emphasizing the group's higher goals and everyone's areas of agreement.

When dealing with a negative person, it's tempting to let yourself slide into anger or frustration. Responding angrily only feeds the negativity. Hold your tongue and listen. Then respond on your terms.

THAT'S SO INSULTING!

At some point in time, we've all been the target of insulting comments. If the insult seems real and not some misguided attempt at a joke, the situation can be hurtful and confusing. Perhaps the person thinks they are being funny but the comment is inappropriate—maybe even offensive, sexist, or racist.

How should you respond in this situation? Many people, when asked, will tell you exactly how they would respond in that situation, but the reality is different. Research shows that there is a discrepancy between what people predict they would do and what they actually do. For this reason, it's worthwhile thinking about the situation in advance and preparing for this eventuality.

Acknowledge or Ignore?

Should you acknowledge the insult or ignore the implication? There are certainly good reasons to acknowledge the comment. You want to preserve your own sense of integrity and signal to the speaker, as well as anyone listening, that this is not OK. Letting the comment go gives them permission to speak in this manner again. At the same time, you might consider the tone of the comment and what the reaction to your response might be. They might be dismissive, *"You're overreacting. It was just a joke,"* or defensive, *"What are you accusing me of?"*

Don't Make Assumptions

Approach the situation as if the person didn't mean to offend you and doesn't realize how their comment is being interpreted. Give them a chance to do the right thing, *"Surely there's another way to say that,"* or *"Did you mean what I think I heard?"* or *"I'm not sure I heard you. Can you please repeat that?"* This will prompt them to think through what they meant by the remark, as well as its effect on others, and give them a chance to take it back or rephrase it on their own.

Instead of immediately labeling the comment as offensive, you might say, *"I know it wasn't your intent, but that description of the project made me uncomfortable."*

You might simply put them on the spot by asking, "*What did you mean by that comment?*" or *"What information are you basing that on?"* By engaging the person in a discussion, you can help them explore their biases and clear up any possible misunderstanding.

Rebalance the Power

People cede power unnecessarily when they allow another individual to make them feel dejected or undermine their work. It's best to change the power dynamic by demonstrating your strength: *"Fortunately, I'm not easily offended."*

Keep your game face on. Don't show the remark has upset you by resorting to anger, welling up in tears, or shouting in reaction. You lose your power when you become too emotional. Again, breathe, stay calm, and respond . . . or not.

People cede power unnecessarily when they allow another individual to make them feel dejected or undermine their work.

As with all thinking-on-your-feet situations, think before you react. Rather than mouthing off with a flip comment you may later regret, take a breath, compose yourself, and concentrate on your professional response.

SUMMARY

Accepting compliments is good for your career. Be proud and say thank you loud and clear. Be proud of yourself and others will share your perspective.

And if you don't know the answers to all the questions, it's OK too. Acknowledge and answer the question based on your own information and professional level. No need to speculate about others; simply be open and candid in your response.

Accept that some people can simply be negative. Don't let their sour tone derail you. Take the high road. Respond with poise and wit and rephrase the discussion with a positive spin. Your response will speak volumes about you. Make it constructive.

MAKE IT REAL WORKSHEETS

Accepting Compliments Is Good for Your Career

Compliments are usually sincere and well-deserved. When you are recognized for a job well done, accepting the compliment testifies to your confidence and the genuine effort you made to do a good job. On the other hand, negating or minimizing the compliment only diminishes your effort and sense of self-worth.

That's why graciously accepting compliments is good for your career. Practice saying "Thank you" and letting it go at that. If you must, provide some supporting information or share the credit with others.

Get in the habit of accepting compliments graciously. Reply to these statements:

"You did an amazing job decorating. The room looks so warm and bright."

"Your presentation was excellent. You'll have to tell me where you found all those great quotes."

"The project turned out better than anyone expected. You did a terrific job motivating your team to keep going in the face of adversity."

____

____

____

____

____

"You are a talented singer. You surprised us all when you sang your personal introduction."

____

____

____

____

____

Don't Let Negativity Derail You

Can't we all just get along? Mostly, yes . . . but not always.

Sometimes people are just negative; other times, there are unrelated issues going on. Whatever the case, the only person's reaction you can control is your own. So, stay focused, stay on track, and remain positive.

It's good to practice some tactics so when the time comes, you're ready.

Restate and reframe. When someone asks, *"Why are you always making excuses for your team?"* You might reframe: *"Are you asking why I am in support of my team even when things are not going well?"*

How would you restate or reframe these comments?

"What were you thinking when you made that disastrous decision?"

"Why do you always choose the most expensive option?"

Probe deeper. When someone makes a negative comment, asking a probing question can often reset their version or encourage their own reframing. For example: *"Why is it so hard to find anything in the storage room?"* You might ask: *"What were you looking for that was not easily accessible?"*

How would you probe deeper to neutralize these comments?

"The numbers you use don't make sense."

"Why do we always choose a dingy color for the tablecloths?"

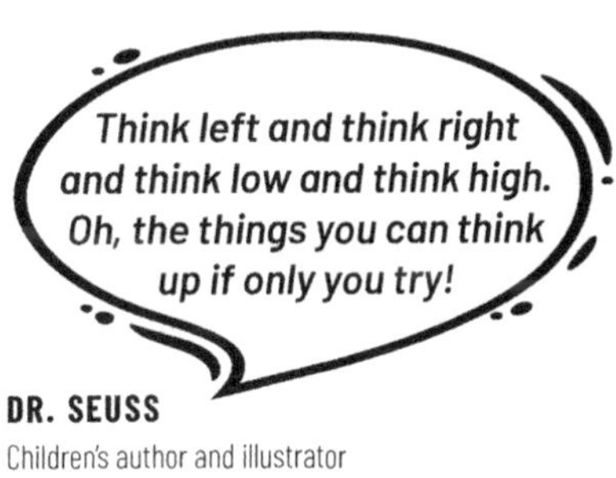

DR. SEUSS
Children's author and illustrator

Chapter 9

The Impromptu Moment

DROP THE MIC!

An **impromptu, or extemporaneous, speech** is a talk that you give on the spot with no preparation. The speech could be as professional as a project update or as casual as a toast at a wedding. Either way, you are expected to say something smart, witty, and charming.

Here are some examples of impromptu speaking opportunities that might arise:

1. Introducing yourself at networking events.
2. Filling in for a late speaker.
3. Giving a toast at a company party.
4. Responding to a question you did not prepare for while on a panel.
5. Fielding unusual job interview questions.
6. Replying to questions from a reporter.
7. Giving an unexpected update to the boss.

8. Responding to unexpected push back on your ideas at a company meeting.
9. Giving a goodbye speech to a departing employee.
10. Responding to a redirected question in the middle of a presentation.

Although unexpected, the impromptu speech should be welcomed as a unique opportunity to become part of the meeting, integral to the discussion, or central to the festivities. This is your chance to share your story and add your perspective. And it's easy when you shift your attention to the audience, speak from the heart, and share what you know.

Shift Attention to the Audience

There are two great reasons to think about the audience immediately. First, it will take your mind's attention off yourself and how nervous or jittery you feel. And second, that's what it's all about: meeting the needs of your audience in this moment.

Who's your audience? What are their interests or concerns? How can you relate to what they are going through? What are their priorities? What are they hoping to hear? Speakers who care about their audience will always have a more fruitful engagement.

In addition, all it takes is a few lines to connect with the audience and make them feel happy you are involved. Tie the department, team, or person with whom you are speaking into your remarks. Draw parallels between the situation you're addressing and the stories or information you share. Mention someone by name, connecting them to the comments you're offering. These are small gestures, but they make your remarks more tailored, meaningful, and relevant.

Stick to the Truth

Tie the department, team, or person with whom you are speaking into your remarks.

No need to embellish, exaggerate, or stretch the facts. The truth is always good enough and key to building trust. For example, if you're asked whether the new process will take more time, be honest: *"It will get harder before it gets easier. But once everyone adjusts, the process will be much more efficient."* Suggesting the new process will immediately solve all problems may sound unlikely and could damage your credibility. If you feel put on the spot, acknowledge it. When you tell the truth, you are authentic.

Make It Personal

When you speak from personal experience, you're referring to things you intimately know. No need to research, no need to investigate, and no need to memorize anything.

When in doubt about what to say, try to tell a story from your past related to the situation. You will sound authentic and your contribution will be unique and valuable.

For example, someone asks you about the Egyptian pyramids, instead of making things up, talk about the time you were in Giza, Egypt, and saw the largest pyramid of all time.

Wait, you never were in Egypt? No problem. Talk about the last time you were talking with your spouse about the Egyptian pyramids.

Wait, you never did that? No problem. Talk about the first time you heard of the pyramids and the other wonders of the world and the impression that made on you.

You get the idea here. No need to make up anything; just look back in your memory to the closest experience with the topic and share it.

Tell a Story to Add Clarity, Humor, and Details When Needed

This sounds like a great idea, but at a moment's notice, this may be hard to come up with. So for this and any other speaking opportunity, it would be great if you had a story or two, in your pocket, lined up and ready to go.

Whether you're at a business meeting, a community event, or a family wedding, you can tell a great story that connects with your audience. Stories are memorable and develop a unique bond with the audience. Refer back to Chapter 7 for ideas on building and telling a great story.

Don't try to be profound. You're not Winston Churchill or Mahatma Gandhi. And that's fine. Be yourself: candid, straightforward, and relatable. You'll sound far more engaging if you speak naturally than if you try to curate every word you say. Relax and speak from the heart.

Be yourself: candid, straightforward, and relatable.

Make eye contact and maintain it. This is true for any speaking situation whether prepared, impromptu, or off the cuff. As we've discussed, eye contact projects confidence and includes the audience in your remarks.

Know you won't be perfect. One of the reasons you may loathe impromptu speaking is because you're terrified of messing up. This is a common theme in Sherry Turkle's book *Reclaiming Conversation: The Power of Talk in a Digital Age*. In it, Turkle explains that many people "actively want to avoid the spontaneity of conversation" and prefer "the edited life" that digital communication now affords us.

But guess what? Everyone makes mistakes. In his book *Forms of Talk*, sociologist Erving Goffman claims that we make a mistake in conversation roughly every 4.6 seconds. So don't hesitate because you're trying to be perfect; you'll be fighting a losing battle.

LESSONS FROM THE BEST COMEBACK LINES OF ALL TIME

Although I promote diplomacy, it's hard to write a book about thinking on your feet without acknowledging some of the best comeback lines of all time.

Comebacks are a rare and fleeting thing, as most of us will only think of the perfect retort to someone hours after we've actually been insulted. Occasionally, however, we can borrow some of the infamous comeback lines of all time to make a point, or get a laugh, or lighten a serious situation.

Here are some for the ages.

"You can't handle the truth."

A Few Good Men (1992)

Lt. Daniel Kaffee finally finds justice, teasing an answer out of Colonel Jessup in the courtroom, but Jessup goes down swinging. When Kaffee asks for the truth, Jessup insists, *"You can't handle the truth."* Of course, while Jessup wins this battle, he loses the war because of it.

Lesson: It's always better not to react in frustration, and sometimes it's best not to respond at all.

"Yippee-ki-yay."

Die Hard (1988)

John McClane single-handedly fights off a group of terrorists and burglars. They try to shoot him down, but in scenes that would make Chumbawamba proud, he gets back up again. Whether it's glass in his feet, a bullet in his arm, or hands around his neck, John just brushes it off and fires back at the bad guys. But the most compelling battle happens over the radio. After taking a radio from the body of a terrorist, John challenges Hans Gruber to a battle of wits. Hans begins to mock John's tough-guy attitude, claiming he's watched too many John Wayne films. Hans asks, *"Do you really think you have a chance against us, Mr. Cowboy?"* To which John calmly responds, *"Yippee-ki-yay."* This comeback line is even better because it returns in the final moments of the film, when John finally takes Hans down in person.

Lesson: Sometimes the path of least resistance is easiest. He calls you a cowboy, so respond like one.

"That's just, like, your opinion, man."

The Big Lebowski (1998)

This Dude is most comfortable staying relaxed and mellow. Nonetheless, he stands up for what he believes in; in this case, that just happens to be fashionable room décor. In the Dude's bowling league, an opposing team threatens to crush them in an upcoming match. This doesn't scare The Dude, however, who responds with a firm and irrefutable comeback: *"That's just, like, your opinion, man."* Fine, it's not a groundbreaking comeback, but what it lacks in creativity, it certainly gains in honesty and brevity.

Lesson: Sometimes a simple response is best, as it leaves little room for further discussion.

"I am serious. And don't call me Shirley."

Airplane! (1980)

Airplane! is filled with witty one-liners, but this one soars above the rest. It's one of the most memorable lines in cinematic history, capturing the pun-filled humor of this absurd satire. Seriously. After the pilots fall ill, the doctor tries to find someone who's both able to fly the plane and hasn't eaten the fish. Luckily, they find Ted, an ex-pilot. After he's asked to fly the plane, Ted tells the doctor, *"Surely you can't be serious."* The doctor offers the famous comeback line, *"I am serious. And don't call me Shirley."*

Lesson: Sometimes a great way to diffuse a situation is with a little humor.

"Frankly, my dear, I don't give a damn."

Gone With The Wind (1939)

Scarlett O'Hara endlessly pursues the love of her life, Ashley Wilkes. But finally, at the end of the four-hour saga, she accepts that it's not going to happen. So Scarlett has to settle for her second choice, Rhett Butler. Unfortunately, Clark Gable's Rhett cannot put up with the whining demands of Scarlett O'Hara anymore. As she questions *"Where shall I go? What shall I do?"* she is met with his cold response, *"Frankly, my dear, I don't give a damn."*

Lesson: You can push other people only so far, until they are no longer interested in pleasing you. Get to the point and be ready to move on.

"I'm gonna make him an offer he can't refuse."

The Godfather (1972)

Nobody turns down the mafia. If the Godfather, Don Corleone (played by Marlon Brando), asks you to cast somebody in a movie, you do it, or you end up with your prize-winning horse's head in your bed. Therefore, it's an offer you can't refuse.

Lesson: If you make a demand, be sure you have the power of consequence.

SUMMARY

When asked to speak on the spot, think first about your audience. What do they care about? What do they want or need to hear? Whether on the spot or planned in advance, always stick to the truth and speak from the heart. Remember, no one is perfect and no one expects you to be perfect either.

MAKE IT REAL WORKSHEETS

Be Ready When You're Called

Impromptu speaking happens to most people more often than they realize. You're asked to say a few words at the spur of the moment and for good or bad, you do.

We can all be better, so why not try? Every opportunity is another chance to impress an audience.

Take a look at these impromptu topics.

Pick at least two and imagine how you might start that conversation with an audience.

My biggest concern for the future is . . .

Real wealth is never measured in money or possessions.

The most important lesson of my life so far . . .

If I ruled the world . . .

Team sports build strong individuals.

In what situation is lying a good idea?

Advertising targeting children is immoral.

The world is a smaller place these days.

Social media makes you less social.

Uniforms stifle individuality.

WARREN BUFFET
Business investor and philanthropist

Chapter 10

Putting It All Together

CONGRATULATIONS!

You've gotten this far, and I hope you learned a lot! You invested in yourself and your ability to think on your feet; to come across with confidence, likeability, and poise; and to make a positive connection with every interaction.

Now You're Ready to Be Ready

Use this book as a reference manual. Come back often, try new strategies, let go of things that don't work. Pick yourself up, dust yourself off after a less-than-stellar experience, and try something different. Don't get overwhelmed. Instead, choose to take small steps; find one idea you think will work and implement it. After you work it and get comfortable applying it, then find another. This will build your confidence and you will naturally start to evolve into the spontaneous, smart, authentic speaker you imagine.

Finding the right techniques to develop your own unique thinking-on-your-feet style is more art than science. Ideally, you want to find the practices that fit best with your personality, experience, and needs. As you encountered the many tips, tricks, and techniques described in this book, you likely felt some would be more helpful than others. Use this as your starting point and initiate small changes in your communication habits.

Finding the right techniques to develop your own unique thinking-on-your-feet style is more art than science.

Once you have established a few new techniques and practices, make an effort to incorporate them into your communication as much as possible. Many of these techniques require practice and patience, but with perseverance, they should help you be more confident, more articulate, and more responsive to your audience.

Now you're ready to be ready for any situation.

Twelve Things to Keep in Mind When Thinking on Your Feet

1. Before you say another word . . . Pause! Excellent speakers know how to use the pause to their advantage. They take a breath, relax, and smile before speaking.

Control the impulse of your subconscious mind. Take a moment to think, collect yourself, and understand the situation before you even begin to respond.

2. Be confident. Look up, breathe deeply, and say something positive to yourself: *"I've got this. I'm smart. They are interested in what I am about to share."*

A confident speaker can be passionate and warm, which fosters connection and respect from his or her audience. Ultimately, your confidence gives you credibility and support for your ideas and initiatives.

3. Focus on the audience. Every presentation or individual discussion needs to be audience centric. They asked the question for a reason. By listening and questioning, you will acknowledge their issue and demonstrate that you understand their concern.

When responding, answer the person, not the question. Try to understand why the question is being asked (concern for budget, time, personal opinion, job security etc.). This knowledge will help you answer appropriately with the right details and perspective.

4. Listen and understand the concern. Actively listening in the moment is the best way to truly understand another person's question, comment, viewpoint, idea, or challenge.

Clarify. Actively listen in the moment, putting your thoughts aside and asking open-ended questions that will uncover the concern; narrow the focus and reframe the question to suit the topic.

5. Use a structure. Help your audience understand your points by choosing a structure that will enhance your response, making it easy for the listener to understand and process.

When you use a structure and apply the Rule of Three, your response comes across as thoughtful, organized, and smart. Your credibility is on the rise.

6. Accept compliments graciously and negativity with resilience. When someone says something nice, simply reply, *"Thank you."* If you absolutely must, add a supportive comment that highlights the experience. This is good for your soul and your career.

Don't let negativity derail you. Try to restate the question or comment in a positive way and respond with kindness and candor. Depersonalize the problems and focus on the issues at hand.

7. Make it a conversation. Imagine you are speaking to close friends and let yourself be authentic and natural. Nobody expects you to know everything.

Use informal language that helps you connect with your audience and feels more inclusive. As your connection with the audience increases, so does your confidence and their trust.

8. Tell a story. Stories engage the audience, evoke empathy, increase trust, and motivate action. Choose a story you know and love so that your authentic, passionate self will naturally emerge.

Tie your story's theme or moral to the point you're trying to make. Help the listener visualize your experience so they can easily make the connection. Your story will be a lasting memory, guaranteed!

9. Demonstrate powerful body language. Standing tall allows you to breathe fully and maximize your voice. In fact, research suggests that people who maximize the full extent of their bodies and the space around them are seen as more powerful and persuasive.

Consider taking one step toward your audience when you begin to speak. Approaching your audience makes you appear confident and welcoming.

10. Use a credible tone of voice. Slow down. Fast talking will increase your discomfort and make it tough for the listener to follow your thoughts. Take your time. Deliver your words and thoughts with precision.

Use assertive words and confident phrases that demonstrate knowledge, experience, and a comfort level with the topic at hand.

11. Use pauses to make an impact. Show confidence with your pause, controlling the conversation by emphasizing key points and allowing your audience time to hear what is being said.

Pauses are both powerful and necessary. Powerful because they show strength on the part of the speaker and necessary to allow the listener to hear and retain the concepts being shared.

12. Breathe. Summarize. Stop. Wrap up your response with a quick summary statement. After that, resist adding more information. End with silence. Let your words stand for themselves.

MAKE IT REAL WORKSHEET

You've Got This

You read the book. You get the concepts. Now it's time for you to find the right combination of skills and techniques that will help you excel at *thinking on your feet.*

Which of these ideas speak most loudly to you? What techniques click and seem natural and easy to do? Those are the ones to try first.

Scan through the book. Look at your notes. Review the exercises you did.

Now, write your own list.

Top 10 Things to Keep in Mind when thinking on my feet.

1. ______________________________

2. ______________________________

3. ______________________________

4. ______________________________

5. ______________________________

6. ______________________________

7. ______________________________

8. ______________________________

9. ______________________________

10. ______________________________

Practice Makes Perfect

Undoubtedly you have noticed that there are **Make It Real Worksheets** at the end of every chapter in this book. And for good reason. Research proves you are more likely to remember and use a new concept if you apply it immediately.

I realize the book's pages are small and so are the worksheets. For this reason, you can download a FREE full-size (8½ x 11) workbook that includes all the worksheets and exercises with plenty of room to think, doodle, and write down your ideas. Simply send an email to me at Dave@humanetricstraining.com requesting a PDF of the workbook, and I'd be happy to provide you with one.

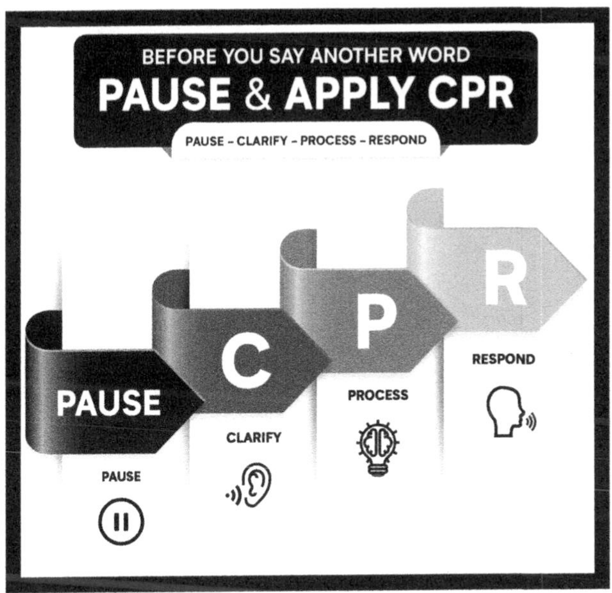

About Dave Minionis, PhD

Organizational Effectiveness Consultant

Dave Minionis is the managing partner of Humanetrics, a global training and consulting firm that specializes in the design and delivery of learning instruments, tools, and programs that build essential personal, interpersonal, and leadership skills. This passionate, professional, and creative consultant has extensive experience in professional and organizational effectiveness. He plays an integral role as a trusted business advisor to many clients.

Dave is an outstanding keynote speaker on topics of change, leadership, and people skills. His knowledge of the topics, entertaining and relevant stories, and humor keep any audience fully engaged.

He consults with organizations and government agencies to determine their specific learning needs and adapts training programs, interventions, and change efforts to fit their unique requirements. His experience in developing leadership competencies, management capabilities, organizational change, and team effectiveness brings a unique perspective to many organizations. Dave helps people evolve, to grow to their full potential. His expert training techniques are known for fostering interactive, engaging, and fun teaching environments.

In addition to his consulting practice, Dave has also been an adjunct professor for both the University of Virginia and George Washington University. At UVA, he taught a leadership series through the school of extended studies; at GWU, he taught a group dynamics course to undergraduates—a class that consistently was rated as one of the most popular on campus.

Dave received his bachelor's degree in psychology at Swarthmore College and received a doctorate in industrial/organizational psychology at George Mason University. His educational background, complimented by his extensive organizational effectiveness experience, provides him with a skill set that is unparalleled. Dave is an asset to any organization.

SPEAKING ENGAGEMENTS

Audiences love to listen, laugh, think, question, and act to improve their lives. That's what happens when Dave is on stage. His keynotes are a great mix of fun and interactive stories of people overcoming life's challenges, eye-opening anecdotes, and surprising researched facts that all serve to move and inspire his audiences in remarkable ways.

Dave speaks on the following topics:

THE MAGIC FORMULA FOR INTERPERSONAL EFFECTIVENESS

Your success may depend to a large degree on how well you interact with others on a daily basis. Because each exchange has the potential of working for or against you in achieving the results you desire, knowing how to communicate effectively in your day-to-day interactions with others is the key to increasing your ability to achieve personal, professional, and organizational success. Dave's presentation uncovers the three essential ingredients to building successful relationships: awareness, ability, and attitude.

BEFORE YOU SAY ANOTHER WORD: Thinking on Your Feet in Moments That Matter Thinking on your feet is a topic that demands audience participation. This entertaining talk includes audience improv, group interaction, and entertaining stories. Conquer your nervousness and sweaty palms with a simple formula for success. Everyone leaves with new and powerful techniques to help resist the temptation to simply react. Learn to respond with poise and confidence to any situation.

Training Solutions

Offered by Dave Minionis and Humanetrics

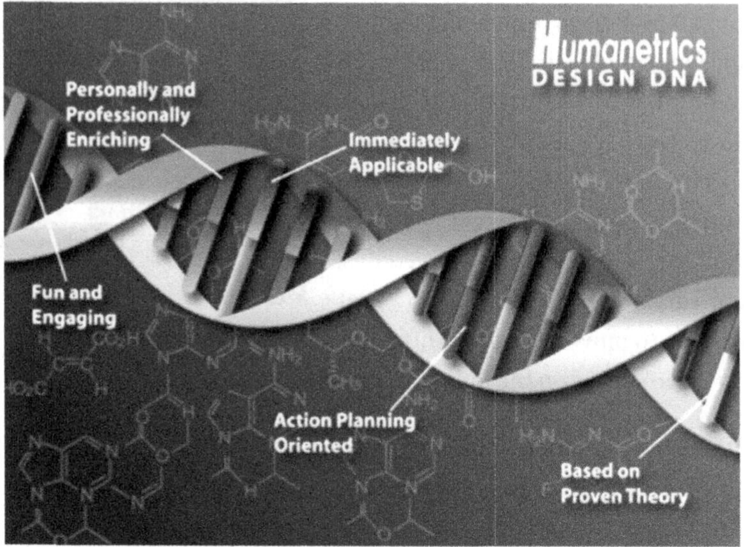

Humanetrics' Design DNA

Dave's unique design DNA makes his learning solutions a fulfilling experience. He believes in a learning that is:

Communicating to Influence

Personal success depends largely on how well people interact with each other. Each interaction has the potential to work for or against achieving the most desirable effect and outcome. Knowing how to communicate effectively and having social intelligence in day-to-day interactions is a critical part of achieving personal and organizational success. ***Communicating to Influence*** is a highly rated program that illuminates how to identify and understand unique behavioral differences among co-workers in ways that enhance relationships and personal performance.

At the end of this program, participants will be able to:

- Understand others and increase **interpersonal effectiveness.**
- **Read others** to **accurately describe** them.
- Manage and **adapt communication** to different situations.
- Leverage **communication strategies** and action plans in their everyday work and personal lives.

Becoming Change Resilient

In today's ever-changing, dynamic environment, it is an absolute given that leaders and their employees need to be prepared to navigate effectively through all the changes going on around them. Although the process or results of change are often viewed as good or bad, change itself is natural and neutral. When we consider the incredible changes the future will bring, it is most important to understand how critical adapting to the impact of those changes will be on our personal and professional health and well-being.

To survive and excel in today's ever-change world, companies need flexible and resilient individuals skilled at riding the many waves of change, as well as leadership at every level that can help move change forward. The most successful organizations take time to teach their employees how to become more change resilient and their leaders how to effectively implement positive change. ***Becoming Change Resilient*** highlights some of the most effective ways to embrace change.

At the end of this program, participants will be able to:

- Recognize the **impact of change**.
- Learn and understand **transition** and the **stages of change**.
- Apply specific **success strategies** to move through each stage of change.
- Lead and **implement change** efforts more effectively.

Persuasive Presentations

Great speakers can be truly inspirational. They are able to connect with their audiences through the delivery of their thoughts, ideas, and messages. They also do something intangible . . . they make us like them, which enables them to keep our attention and influence others. ***Persuasive Presentations*** delivers the knowledge and working exercises on how to be a successful communicator—in stand-up presentations, business meetings, sales calls, and everyday interactions.

At the end of this program, participants will be able to:

- Leverage their skills and talents to **deliver a winning presentation**.
- Use techniques and planning structuring to **organize and present ideas persuasively**.
- Adapt a presentation to the **needs of their audience**.
- Effectively use **presentation aids and stories** to get impact.
- Improve delivery through master coaching **feedback and personal exercises**.

Thinking on Your Feet in Moments That Matter

Professionals are consistently put on the spot while attending a meeting, presenting a proposal, selling ideas, or answering questions in everyday conversations. Articulating one's thoughts, being able to improvise in the moment, and thinking on one's feet in unanticipated situations is a critical skill set professionals use to excel and leaders use to influence. The most successful and admired business professionals come across as confident, competent, and in control. They seem to know exactly what words to use before they communicate and respond to others. They answer questions smoothly and with confidence. Speaking "off the cuff" is a unique skill, and it can improve with training and practice.

The workshop ***Thinking on Your Feet in Moments That Matter*** will help participants master the ability to communicate in the moment with confidence, credibility, and flexibility during high-stakes interactions. Built on key fundamentals of persuasive presentations, this highly engaging workshop delivers the knowledge and tactics to successfully communicate in stand-up presentations, business meetings, and everyday interactions.

At the end of this program, participants will be able to:

- **Organize their thoughts** into a quality presentation that is clear, concise, and memorable.
- **Adapt to curveballs** quickly during meetings and key interactions.
- Develop **professional presence** by being able to improvise in different situations.
- **Clarify, process, and respond** to unexpected comments or reactions in the moment.

Thinking about Thinking

Top organizations today continue to find ways to improve employee effectiveness, increase inclusion, and reduce negative stereotypes and biases in the workplace. We now have a much better understanding of how the human mind works. By getting people to "think about how they think" and become ***more aware of their unconscious biases***, as well as ***creating a growth mindset***, we can fostermore healthy and productive work environments.

The program ***Thinking about Thinking*** will get participants to start thinking about how their brains work. It will help them consciously reflect on them unconscious minds. By doing so, they will be more aware of biases and mindset, which will help improve their decision-making and productivity.

At the end of this program, participants will be able to:

- Become aware of **unconscious biases** in the workplace.
- Develop strategies for **managing against biases**.

- Explain the crucial **role of mindset** to effectiveness.
- Articulate the **benefits of a growth mindset** vs fixed mindset.
- Choose more empowering **growth mindset language**.
- Highlight the importance of **inclusion** in the workplace,

Team Peak Performance

Over the last several decades, we have seen an increased interest in teamwork. Companies have had to do more with less. Organizations have used teams to get projects done faster and better. But just because you throw a bunch a people together does not mean you are going to get a high-performing team. Many teams fail to get off the ground, while others that do, crash along the way. Creating and maintaining effective teams takes careful planning and systematic monitoring.

Team Peak Performance is an experiential workshop designed to accelerate team development. It balances essential "best practice" content with active participant involvement. It contains everything needed to help teams accelerate their progress into the unknown, including:

- Best practices and applicable team theory.
- Instructional materials designed to help teams overcome road-blocks to their effectiveness.
- Experiential exercises.

At the end of this program, participants will be able to:

- Understand the **characteristics of a high performing team**.
- Describe the **phases of team development** so they can help their team perform better.
- Magnify their effectiveness by concentrating on the **critical components** essential to high-performing teams
- **Create high-performing teams**.

Made in the USA
Monee, IL
14 November 2020